More Praise for Invest like a Dealmaker

Chris Mayer is one of the few people in America who thinks deeply and originally about investing. The ideas in this book will enrich you and change your perspective about investing forever. You'll never look at a stock symbol in the same way. This is the complete guide to sophisticated, safe investing.

—Porter Stansberry, founder, *Stansberry & Associates Investment Research*

I've known Chris for years now. His new book has all the essential principles of investing, historical vignettes about curious characters and insights from all the greatest investing legends, tied up in an entertaining package that only someone as well-read as Chris could produce. In the last twenty years, I've read hundreds of financial books. Most weren't worth the time it took to read the table of contents. You'll want to read *Invest Like a Dealmaker* cover to cover and refer to it often.

—Dan Ferris, editor, *Extreme Value*

Chris Mayer has put together a wonderful compendium of investment wisdom. You'll find the "usual suspects"—Warren Buffett, Jay Gould, George Soros, et al. But you'll also learn from great investors you've never heard of, backed up with great research. Turn to just about any page and you'll find something profound that will help you make more money in the markets.

—Mark Tier, author, *The Winning Investment Habits of Warren Buffett & George Soros*

This excellent book by Chris Mayer, an accomplished securities analyst, can be read in three hours. But it contains so many interesting observations supported by the investment knowledge of some of the world's most successful value investors that every reader will gain insights that will serve him well for the rest of his life!

—Marc Faber, editor, the *Gloom Boom & Doom Report*

Chris Mayer has done a nice job of explaining and illustrating how and why a company (and its stock) can be valued differently by people who simply view it through different perspectives. His book is a useful addition to the library on investing.

—Ron Muhlenkamp, president, Muhlenkamp & Company, Inc.

INVEST LIKE A DEALMAKER

INVEST LIKE A DEALMAKER

Secrets from a Former Banking Insider

CHRISTOPHER W. MAYER

Foreword by Addison Wiggin

John Wiley & Sons, Inc.

Published by John Wiley & Sons, Inc., Hoboken, New Jersey.
Published simultaneously in Canada.

Wiley Bicentennial Logo: Richard J. Pacifico

Quoted material from interview with Martin Whitman reprinted from "Value at Risk," by James Grant, *Grant's Interest Rate Observer* 24, no. 21 (November 23, 2006). Reprinted with permission of Grant's, copyright 2007.

For general information on our other products and services or for technical support, please contact our Customer Care Department within the United States at (800) 762-2974, outside the United States at (317) 572-3993 or fax (317) 572-4002.

Wiley also publishes its books in a variety of electronic formats. Some content that appears in print may not be available in electronic formats. For more information about Wiley products, visit our Web site at www.wiley.com.

Library of Congress Cataloging-in-Publication Data:

Mayer, Christopher W., 1972–
    Invest like a dealmaker : secrets from a former banking insider/
  by Christopher W. Mayer.
        p.   cm.
    Includes bibliographical references and index.
    ISBN 978-0-470-18091-4 (cloth)
        1. Stocks.   2. Corporations—valuation.   3. Portfolio management.
    4. Investments.   I. Title.
    HG4661.M375   2008
    332.63'22—dc22

                                                                    2007034460
Printed in the United States of America.

10 9 8 7 6 5 4 3 2 1

CONTENTS

FOREWORD

WHEN COOLER HEADS PREVAIL

In July of 2007, the U.S. financial markets spawned a global panic. Spurious loans made for years in U.S. "subprime mortgage" markets, repackaged and pawned off with triple AAA ratings to unsuspecting retirement planners, regressed to their natural value: zero. The revelation at such funds as the Bear Stearns High-Grade Structured Credit Strategies Fund and the High-Grade Structured Credit Strategies Enhanced Leverage Fund, sent shock waves through investment markets around the globe.

Although it had taken weeks to determine the funds' values, and even after Bear Stearns put over $3.2 billion to bail out these funds (the largest bailout by a bank in about a decade), investors were told they'd get little or nothing back on their investments. Put another way, the funds were practically worthless and billions of dollars went up in smoke.

In the ensuing months, credit markets tightened. And market volatility increased. The financial system, in a word, went haywire. In a speech before the Brookings Institution, Alan Greenspan, former chairman to the Federal Reserve, likened the crisis to those that happened not only in recent U.S. history in 1987 and 1998 . . . but all the way back to 1837 and 1907.

As of this writing, possibly even when you read this, the end of the contraction and the depth of this particular episode in market folly are still unknown. But for a stretch in the August heat, there wasn't an investor in the world who wasn't concerned about the value of their stock holdings.

During one 56 hour period, after the largest bank in Europe, BNP Paribas, admitted they too would have to restate $2.3 billion in subprime exposure markets started selling off in Europe. France's benchmark index, shed nearly 2 percent. Deutschland followed. The DAX was down 1.6 percent. Even the Brits felt the sting . . . the FTSE 100 lost 1.5 percent. In fact, not a single European market was safe . . . all 18 exchanges fell. Then it spread to the United States, then Asia.

The sell-off was only partially stymied by $146 billion dollars in "liquidity" injected into the banking system: $130 billion by the ECB, $12 billion by the Federal Reserve, $4 billion more by the Bank of Australia.

Also, during the panic, many investors, advisors and pundits lost their heads. In one episode made famous by multiple downloads on YouTube, Jim Cramer, founder of TheStreet.com and host of CNBC's Mad Money, screamed pound-fisting mad for Ben Bernanke, chairman of the Federal Reserve, to "stop acting like an academic and do something." There was "Armageddon on Wall Street" he screamed at his interviewer . . . continuing long after her subtle urging to settle down.

I was working at the time on a pet project for readers of our investment newsletters called the *5 Min. Forecast.* We were trying to tie events in the daily stock news into larger trends we saw developing, and help readers either avoid them, in the case of the subprime fiasco, or take advantage of them, as in the literally billions of dollars being thrown at the alternative energies industry in the wake of another panic popular with the press at the time: Global Warming.

During those manic months of the Panic of 2007, Chris Mayer remained calm, objective, even philosophical. He cautioned readers of his newsletter Capital & Crisis and subsequently those who read the *5 Min. Forecast,* to "Stay focused on what you own and why you own it. If your reasons for owning something are still valid, you should hang on." And on another occasion he suggested: "When the market starts selling everything off indiscriminately, there are bound to be opportunities in the aftermath. I think that in the still-warm ashes of a market sell-off there are goodies to be found. I'm committed to finding them. Over the longer term, I'm betting we'll be happy we held onto many of our stocks." Of course, he was right. But it was not what you heard many people saying while the panic was unfolding.

It wasn't a reaction to what was happening in the global markets so much as an adherence to hard-learned, strict and often difficult to sustain principles of investing. The book you're about to read is an in-depth guide to understanding Chris Mayer's investing principles. Before we delve into what they are, let me tell you how he fared during the panic: His 17 open recommendations in Capital & Crisis still averaged gains of close to 40 percent. He had no subprime exposure, or mortgage lending exposure at all. No homebuilders and no funky credit strategy funds. He didn't have to sell any of his holdings. Chris had his readers in some of the best places you could be in such a crisis. His companies were loaded with cash and assets and often had long-term powerful trends behind them.

Compared to many other portfolios, his sailed through cleanly.

Chris' investment principles come from two distinct places: an earnest desire to learn from the masters and a dedication to detail, hard-wrought from his experience as a commercial banker at two prestigious banks: Riggs Bank of Washington, DC, the bank of presidents (since acquired by PNC Financial), and Provident Bank, of Baltimore, MD. During his tenure as a corporate lender, Chris never lost money on a single deal. Even when things didn't work out, the bank got its money back because of his careful due diligence and insistence on asset quality. Chris became a Vice President while only in his twenties—a rare feat—and he handled high-stake negotiations for hundreds of millions of dollars in loans.

Early in this book, Chris lays out the core principle behind the investment strategy that served him so well during his years in banking. Two markets exist for stocks, says Chris, or more specifically, for businesses. There is the market of public quotations—the prices you see quoted on Yahoo! Finance—which most investors know very well.

But, there is also a private market—a market for the control of a company—which is every bit as real. Most investors pay attention only to the first, and ignore—if they are even aware of—the second. Yet, some of the best investment opportunities exist when there are wide disparities between these two markets. For example, Chris recently recommended a little oil services company called T-3 Energy Services at around $21 per share. As he pointed out to his readers: "I don't think T-3 will trade at current prices for very long. At these prices, it makes for a solid acquisition target." He showed his readers how energy companies had bought comparable companies at prices that implied a double for T-3. Only 4 months later, T-3 hit $36 per share—a 70 percent gain for his readers. And it was based on a relatively simple insight. Dealmakers in the private market were paying a lot more to own companies like T-3 than the price stock market gave them.

Recognizing this core tenet of investing puts you, in one easy step, light-years ahead of the average "punter." But that's only the beginning. In *Invest Like a Dealmaker,* Mr. Mayer divulges the "big ideas" any investor needs, be they individual or professional, to earn money over the long run.

For example, how do you think about risk? Most investors think risk means the stock price going down. But Chris shows you why that's a mistake and how the truly great investors never think that way. Why? Because they anchor their valuations in this other private market. They know the real value of a business is not what the stock market says it is. It can be very different. And what do you truly understand about the "principles of wealth creation"? Most investors have a rather myopic view of how businesses create wealth. Mainly, investors think it is all about earnings or perhaps the stock price itself. *Invest Like a Dealmaker* explores the many ways in which companies create true wealth. Once you realize the full menu of options available, it will change the way you assess whether a stock is attractive or not.

After you've nailed these principles, Mayer will guide you to the most fertile hunting grounds for good companies, good stocks; the very places you're most likely to find winners. At the end of the day, this book should prove to be a deep well of ideas for you draw from for years to come. Over time, you'll develop your own favorite variations on these themes and ideas. But that is as it should be. Investing is a fluid process with new ideas adding to the mix all the time.

That's also why, as an astute student of markets, Chris has opted to regale you with the ideas and insights of some of the most accomplished investors and thinkers of our time and the recent past. Unlike other books, Chris doesn't give you their life story. He delivers the meat: their most important insights, the essential takeaways from at least a half-dozen great money managers and investment strategists. You'll be pleasantly surprised to learn that some of the most important lessons come from names you've likely never heard before.

In many ways, investing is not about when to buy, but when to sell. Nearly all investment books, even the good ones, deal with when to sell in a few paragraphs. Selling is never easy. Chris has devoted a chapter to this part of the investing process. You'll appreciate the results, as he divulges a sound and smart selling strategy—used by some of the greats.

Not to mention a cautionary word about the pitfalls to avoid. There are many. A core tenet of this book is that the secret to successful long-term investing is avoiding serious losers. But by following the principles outlined here, you'll gain exactly the kind of confidence that you'll need to prevail when markets get jittery as they did in July and August of 2007, or better yet, to succeed wildly when bull markets prevail.

Chris Mayer and I first met in person at the Red, Hot and Blue barbecue joint in Laurel, Maryland. We enjoyed a plate of ribs, some cold beers, and a taste of the blues. We'd made an acquaintance several years before by e-mail correspondence, but at that restaurant a true friendship was born.

Chris is as down to earth as the surroundings in which we first met. He's literate, hard-working, and honest. You could do a whole lot worse than understand the investment strategies described in this book. And I'm confident many investors will.

—Addison Wiggin

ACKNOWLEDGMENTS

I would like to thank Addison Wiggin, our fearless leader at Agora Financial. He has been a tireless supporter of my work and a good friend. Thanks also to Eric Fry for his many words of wisdom and encouragement over the years.

Every writer owes many unpaid debts to countless people who have helped along the way. I can only acknowledge some of them here, but the list is surely longer. Thanks to all my friends at Agora Financial for their help and support: William Bonner, Shauna Zarrin, Greg Grillot, John Forde, Danielle Morino, and Joe Shriefer. And to my friends at S&A—Porter Stansberry, Steve Sjuggerrud, Dan Ferris, and Brian Hunt. Thanks also to my old high school buddy and now doctor, M. Samir Qamar, who provided helpful comments and never fails to sing my praises. And to Eric Winig for all those talks over coffee and the good ideas that came from them.

Also, the team at Wiley was easy to work with and efficient. Thanks, in particular, to Todd Tedesco and Stacey Small.

I would also like to acknowledge my family members who have always been pillars of encouragement, always overlooking my flaws, and cheering me on. Thanks, especially, to my mom and dad. Finally, I could never have written this book without the love and support of my wife Carol.

CHAPTER 1

A TALE OF TWO MARKETS

When I finally go to stand on this spot, it just reaffirmed a lot of my beliefs about what good investing is all about. Stocks are more than just ticker symbols. They represent companies that exist in the real world of blood and sweat and tears. They have real assets that you can touch and smell and count and, in this case, walk on.

I was in Buenos Aires, Argentina, standing on some of the most valuable raw land remaining in the city—a parcel of land called Santa Maria del Plata. It was a beautiful day. The sky was a cornflower blue with big puffy white clouds and a bright yellow sun. A soft breeze blew in from the brown waters of the Rio de la Plata.

In the background, you could see the busy cranes at work in nearby Puerto Madero—a revitalized port now lined with shops and cafés, with tall office buildings making up a sparkling skyline. A five-minute cab ride and you could be in downtown Buenos Aires.

It was a great location. If you look at an aerial map of Buenos Aires down near the river, you can see two significant areas of green. One is a park and preserve. The Argentines will never develop it. The second, though, is this piece of property I stood on. The future of Buenos Aires development was right here.

In October 2006, only four months before I visited Argentina, I recommended the shares of the company that owned this land, Investments and Representations, or IRSA for short. The value implied in this land, based on what private buyers and sellers were paying, more than covered the value of the stock in the public market. And IRSA owned lots of shopping centers, hotels, office property, and more. It was like getting the land for free.

By April 2007, the stock was up more than 40 percent. It's nice to have quick confirmation of an investment thesis.

The key insight here was simply that what was trading in the stock market—the value of IRSA's stock—did not reflect adequately the value of its assets in the private market. In other words, private buyers looking to buy the whole company would have paid a lot more than what the stock market valued IRSA's stock at.

Finding those key insights means focusing on things most investors don't focus on. Heck, most investors would never see the value of IRSA's land. It doesn't show up on an earnings statement. There's no easy way to troll for it with a computer stock screen. To discover the value of IRSA's land, investors would have to think about stocks and wealth creation in a whole different way. They would need to focus on assets and compare the value of those assets in the stock market to their value in the private market. Two markets—the public one and the private one.

I go to great lengths to uncover these kinds of deals for readers of my newsletter, *Capital & Crisis*. What I hope this book will show you is how to think about stock market values. I'll give you a framework to think about and to use and build on. You won't have to hop on a plane and go anywhere. You can start using this framework right away from your own home.

And along the way we'll cover a lot of what investment greats have done, how they did it, and the useful nuggets we can take from them. I call them "dealmakers." *Dealmakers are people who think about stocks as whole companies, as things with real assets and cash flows that exist in the real world.*

As it turns out, this idea is part of an old playbook used throughout history. . . .

COBBLESTONES, BEER, AND BROKEN PROMISES

Jay Gould, a nineteenth-century investor, became very rich as a speculator and owner of companies. What was his secret? What was his special insight? And more importantly, is that insight something we can use today?

Gould began his career in the tannery business. He had bad timing, though, because shortly after he got started the country had another panic, and the tannery business suffered. Leather prices plummeted, and profit margins tightened.

But he didn't sell out, which is what most investors would do. Most investors have a habit of selling what's gone down and buying what's gone up. The dealmakers of the world almost never do.

In fact, Gould bought out his partner, his first big coup. It's amazing how many fortunes get started by buying stuff that no one else seems to want and hanging on until things get better. Of course, there is much more to it than that, just as there is more to a good recipe than the ingredients alone. You need to know how to use them or you wind up with a disaster in the kitchen. Investing is like that if you don't know what you are doing.

Wall Street in Gould's day was certainly no place for the unprepared. As Henry Clews observed in the first of his two memoirs:

> The road to Hell is not—contrary to popular opinion—paved with good intentions. It is instead paved with cobblestones, beer and broken promises. That is Wall Street, plain and simple, the place where the faithless mingle, where dreams are shattered and fortunes lost and made.[1]

That's still a pretty good description.

Gould, though, learned how to play the game. He immersed himself in studying the seasoned financiers of his day, reading financial newspapers and other material with religious dedication. It wasn't long before he reaped his first big payday, purchasing the bonds of the Rutland & Washington Railroad for 10 cents on the dollar. The R&W was a struggling line, and dirt-cheap.

In less than two years he sold it and made more than 10 times his money, netting over $100,000—a huge amount in those days. Not even 30 years old, he was well on his way to becoming one of Wall Street's most successful players.

Now, what do we make of his story?

Charlie Munger, the witty and sometimes bitingly sarcastic—and funny—sidekick to Warren Buffett, likes to say, "There are answers worth billions of dollars in a thirty-dollar history book."

I believe him. History may be an abstract teacher, but it teaches profitable lessons nonetheless. "Hindsight enhances foresight," as James Grant, editor of the well-regarded eponymous newsletter *Grant's*, put it.

Munger says this because the old formula still works—buy what's cheap and hang on. But before you can understand what's cheap, you have to understand something investors like Gould—and many others—have long understood. It's how Gould knew the R&W was a good buy.

It is the tale of two markets.

There are two markets for stocks. I'm not talking about exchanges, like the NASDAQ or the NYSE. And I'm not talking about markets for stocks in the United States versus the market in London or some other seemingly faraway place.

I'm talking about two distinct markets whose prices for the same goods, or stocks, can vary widely at times. This variability, as you might imagine, creates opportunities for knowing investors.

The fact that two markets exist has a profound consequence for investors. It's a fact that we're going to vet thoroughly in this chapter. Indeed, since it forms one of the cornerstones of my entire approach to investing, we better lay it out early so that the rest of this book will make sense.

It's so important that you may never look at a stock quote in quite the same way after you read this section.

To be more precise when I talk about two markets, I'm really referring to two markets for businesses. Stocks, remember, represent shares of a business. The newspapers print the quotes from one market every day. It's also the one you can look up by going online and getting a stock quote. That's one market.

But there is another market. This market consists of private transactions or transactions for whole businesses. A meaningful transaction is taking place any time one business buys another, and you should pay attention to it.

The papers don't print these prices in their stock tables, and you can't get them off the Internet quote systems. Yet they are every bit as real as the publicly reported stock prices.

Most people don't appreciate this fact, so they give undue weight to the first market. That's the one they can easily see. That's the one that counts when they go to buy and sell. Well, these people are making a mistake in my view. Benjamin Graham thought so, too.

Graham was one of the most important figures in investing in the twentieth century. He is widely known as the dean of security analysis. As Adam Smith (a.k.a. George Goodman) once wrote: "The reason that Graham is the undisputed dean is that before him there was no profession and after him they began to call it that."[2] His books and writings were influential in teaching many how to invest. One of his disciples was Warren Buffett.

In *The Intelligent Investor*, Graham asserts that a true investor would be better off without market quotations on his stock market holdings. He writes: "[The investor] would then be spared the mental anguish caused him by other persons' mistakes of judgment."[3] What did the great master mean by this? I think he was referring to the concept of two markets, or two prices, for the same stock.

Let me explain more about this concept.

THE REALITY OF PUBLIC QUOTATIONS

Most investors reading this book buy and sell stocks based on public quotations. If you want to buy 1,000 shares of Maltese Falcon Financial (I love those old Bogart movies!), you can do this very easily these days. You probably log on to your online broker, punch in the ticker MFF (I'm making this up by the way), and in seconds have your order filled. It's all very easy.

You now have your 1,000 shares, which you could just as easily sell. Let me note a few things about your position at this moment:

1. You are a minority owner in Maltese Falcon Financial, an enterprise the market values at $1 billion.
2. You are a passive owner in that you have no control or substantial influence over how the company is run or how it uses its assets—beyond the voting power of your 1,000 shares.
3. You are an outsider, meaning that you are not privy to all the information to which management is privy.

You are what is called in the trade an "outside passive minority" (OPM) investor. Although that phrase is sort of cumbersome, it's a literal description of your position.

But your reality is not the only reality. Remember the old bit about Plato's cave? He posited that we are all like people in a cave with a fire burning behind us as we sit looking at the shadows cast on the wall of the cave. What we see is but one reality.

Or to put it in other terms, in the investing world you are either a passenger or a driver. The OPMI is a passenger.

Now consider the other market for the same shares in the same company. This example is simplified to make a specific point. Here it is:

Let's say Vulcan Asset Management wants to take a position in Maltese Falcon Financial (I just made up that name, though indeed there may be some new fund calling itself that).

Vulcan likes to take big bets and get involved in the companies it invests in. The guys at Vulcan think there is some hidden value in Maltese Falcon, and they feel management is not doing all it could do to realize that value. Vulcan has some ideas of its own that Maltese Falcon should pursue. Namely, Vulcan thinks that the big slug of cash in Maltese Falcon's bank account should be used to buy back stock and that this would be the best use of Maltese's cash because such buybacks will give the share price a kick in the pants.

So Vulcan starts to invest in the stock in pieces over several months. Unlike you, a company can't buy all it wants at one time or the price would go through the roof. Let's say Vulcan wants to buy $200 million worth of stock. If it buys its whole $200 million investment at no more than $40 per share, it will still need to accumulate 5 million shares. On a typical day, Maltese Falcon trades, let's say, 400,000 shares. So even if Vulcan picks up 100,000 shares a day, it will still take the company 50 days to get all it wants.

Then, too, once Vulcan buys 5 percent of Maltese Falcon, it has to file with the Securities and Exchange Commission (SEC) and publicly disclose the purchase. Now, regular folks like you and me can read about it in *Barron's* under the section titled "13-D filings." Not only that, but Vulcan's competitors can see what they're doing. All of this could affect the market price even more, especially if Vulcan has something of a reputation. When Warren Buffett buys a partial interest in just about anything, it gets written up in newspapers and magazines.

Basically, it gets thoroughly aired out in public and the price soars, making it difficult for Buffett to get any more at his price. (Most recently, Burlington Northern rose 6 percent after Buffett disclosed he had bought the stock.)

So this procedure must be a nuisance for folks like those at Vulcan, who would just love to get their full position nice and quiet.

But let's say they get their full position in, and now they own their 5 million shares or so at an average price of just under $40. That makes Vulcan the largest shareholder in Maltese Falcon Financial. Let's say it owns 20 percent of the shares outstanding. Now management has to pay attention to Vulcan, which has some clout. It can make things happen in a proxy contest by nominating different members of the board of directors, which then can change the management team around. Vulcan can put forth different resolutions for the company to abide by. In short, it has some measure of control or influence over what happens at Maltese Falcon Financial.

INSIDE INVESTORS VERSUS OUTSIDE INVESTORS

Now let's consider Vulcan's position:

1. It is the largest single shareholder of Maltese Falcon Financial.
2. It is an active owner with some control and influence over how the company's assets are deployed.
3. It is an insider. It is privy to information and contact with management that outside owners don't have access to.

Moreover, unlike the guy with his 1,000 shares, Vulcan is not able to easily sell its shares. If it started dumping its shares, there would be a massive fall in price, and Vulcan's investment capital would be greatly impaired.

So let's summarize the differences between the two types of investors.

Instead of an outside passive minority investor, Vulcan is an inside, active, (near-) majority investor. That position is a different thing altogether, as you can readily see. There is a substantial difference between our first investor holding 1,000 shares and Vulcan.

Conversely, we might just have Vulcan buy the whole company. Let's say Vulcan makes a $40 per share cash bid on Maltese Falcon Financial, which is a 25 percent premium over the quoted market price of $32 per share.

The management team at Maltese takes the offer to the board of directors, and then they decide to put it up for vote among the shareholders. The shareholders accept the offer. The deal closes six months later, and Maltese becomes a wholly owned subsidiary of Vulcan. The ticker MFF is retired, and shareholders get $40 in cash for every share of Maltese they own.

Now the question is, why would Vulcan do that? Why would it be willing to pay up to 25 percent more than the publicly quoted price?

Well, here is where things get very interesting. . . .

Let's say that Maltese has a market value on the public markets of about $1 billion and it has no debts. In our investing approach, we call this value an enterprise value (EV), a concept familiar to many professionals and enthusiasts but not so widely used by casual investors or even media types. Basically, enterprise value is the theoretical price you would have to pay to purchase the whole business. Unlike simply looking at the market cap, EV also considers the value of debts. (I'll get into more detail about this concept and the art of valuation later.)

Let's say Maltese was trading for an EV-to-EBITDA (earnings before interest, taxes, depreciation, and amortization) ratio of only four times. The average investor usually talks in terms of price–earnings ratios, but the dealmaker almost never does. Again, I'll say more about this later, but just hang with me here for a minute. For now, you can think of EV-to-EBITDA as akin to a price earnings ratio, a term you are probably more familiar with. Low EV-to-EBITDA implies cheapness, and a higher ratio would imply a pricier stock—which would mean you're simply paying more per dollar of pretax earnings.

Let's also say that Vulcan knows that in the private markets companies like Maltese have been bought and sold at multiples of nine times EV-to-EBITDA. These transactions occurred with private companies. They were mostly family-owned businesses or local institutions that were bought and sold by other private companies and investors.

In any event, an EV-to-EBITDA of five for Maltese (after paying a 25 percent premium over the public market price) looks pretty darn cheap to Vulcan. So Vulcan thinks that it is getting a great deal and that, if it wanted to, it could take Maltese and sell it into this private market and make an 80 percent gain easily on its purchase price. Because, again, the private market valuation is nine times, versus only the five times Vulcan paid. Buy for five and sell for nine. Believe it or not, you can find deals like this in the stock market—that's what this book is about. And that's what I do for a living—find disparities like this for my reader-investors.

In the meantime, Vulcan can run the company, pursue its strategies, and enjoy the privileges and benefits that come from owning a company.

This last point is important. The issue of control has an impact on price. Normally, you'd be willing to pay more for a business you can control versus one in which you are simply a minority investor. Control, however, is not always a plus. When you buy an entire business, owning that business entails responsibilities as well (paying taxes, following rules and regulations, and so on), some of which may be more hassle than they are worth. Contrary to popular belief, a stock may not be worth owning at any price—especially if claims against it exceed the value of the business.

But to get back to our Vulcan and Maltese example. . . .

THE PROFIT OPPORTUNITY BETWEEN
THE TWO MARKETS

Now, you might say: "Well, why the heck would Maltese accept the offer?"

In reality, they might not. Management would argue strenuously that the business is worth much more than that. But the other shareholders are not so sure and think maybe management just wants to keep their plush jobs at the company. Most of the shareholders are regular people like our fellow who owns 1,000 shares. Or they are institutional investors—mutual fund managers—who need to beat their benchmarks and don't want to wait around. A 25 percent quick gain looks good to these kinds of investors, so they accept it. Maybe management likes the deal, too, because they are getting older and want to get paid out on their stock options. There could be lots of reasons. People make bad deals all the time in business.

Of course, management could have taken matters into their own hands a bit sooner. Maybe they should have taken that wad of cash and bought back stock—a great investment given how cheap their company looked compared to private market deals. Maybe they could have banded together and bought the company themselves and taken it private. They could have sought out a more favorable deal. Lots of things could have happened.

In this example, I made the public company the cheap one. But it can happen the other way around, too. Maybe the public company's shares are valued at nine times EBITDA, and the private companies are valued at only five. Then what happens is different. Then the private companies want public stock so that they, too, can get the windfall of profits at nine times EBITDA versus only five.

In this instance, private companies similar to Maltese will go public. There will be an initial public offerings boom in these companies, and investors will snap up shares. Conversely, the public companies may use their richly valued shares to purchase private companies outright.

But the bottom line—and the most important fact I want to establish early—is that there are two markets for stocks. Stock market prices, as quoted in newspapers and online sites, prevail in one market. And that market is tethered to another market normally made up of private and well-informed buyers and sellers.

(I say "normally," but you should not automatically assume that private market values are always the "correct" ones. Most of the time, private transactions involve knowledgeable buyers and sellers, whereas in the public markets prices can be set by millions of Joe Blow investors who suddenly think it's a cool thing to own an Internet company or an oil company or whatever is hot at the moment.)

Much of the approach in this book is playing an arbitrage between these two markets. In other words, buying public companies when they appear undervalued versus private market values.

The difficulty is that private market values are not always easily obtainable. It often takes some digging. Plus, some businesses are easier to value than others. Some businesses are unique and involve so many different parts that it's hard to value them with private market comparables. Sometimes private market comparables are just not available and you have to make some estimate of what an intelligent buyer might pay for the whole company you are looking at.

None of this should be at all surprising. If valuation were easy, investing would be easy, too. And we know that it's not so easy. But later in this book, I'm going to show you some excellent places to look for bargains and some shortcuts you can use to think like a dealmaker.

THINK LIKE A DEALMAKER

Marty Whitman is one of my favorite investors, and you'll hear more from him in the pages that follow. He runs the Third Avenue Value Fund and has been in the business for over 50 years. He's got a great track record, and his shareholder letters (and books) are loaded with investment insights and wisdom.

On the two-market concept, Whitman writes:

> These two disparate markets exist for the same commodity—common stocks. That valuations ordinarily should be different between these two markets seems obvious. After all, when valuing whole businesses the standards of analysis and the decision considerations tend to be different than when trying to predict open-market stock prices.[4]

The reality of the two different markets also means that the outside passive minority investors and the inside active control investors ("the dealmakers") have very different standards and other considerations they use to value businesses. Indeed, the dealmakers are conceptualizing those two markets in a different way.

Part of my recommendation to you is that you adopt this dealmakers' way of looking at things as much as you practically can. These ideas are the basis of the approach I follow personally and in my newsletter *Capital & Crisis*. Let's look at some of the ways in which dealmakers differ from typical outside passive minority investors.

WHAT'S MORE IMPORTANT TO YOU AS A CONTROL INVESTOR?

The control investors care more about the long term. After all, they are going to buy a business or take a large interest in a business, and as we've seen, they can't leave either of these positions very easily. This forces them to think more about the long term. What is the long term? It is usually a period of at least several years.

When control investors look to buy a business, they care less about the immediate performance and more about the long-term performance. They are cognizant of the risk of overpaying for a star that has one good year. In my banking career, we always looked back at how a business had performed over a period of several years to get a sense of how it performed in a variety of environments and conditions.

Control investors care more about the whole picture of the business and are not fixated on earnings per share. Companies may own other assets that make them attractive to own (like IRSA with all of its raw land). Or they may have certain liabilities that make them less attractive. The dealmaker looks at the quality and quantity of resources in a business and thinks about what can be done with them. The dealmaker's focus is on building wealth.

Perhaps the most important point about thinking like a dealmaker is that it gives you a different perspective on the stock prices quoted in newspapers and available on your computer. You know a little about how those prices come about, and knowing this, you may understand why many great investors tend to view market prices not as something to predict but as something to take advantage of.

Think back to the Ben Graham quote at the beginning of this chapter. He wrote that investors would be better off without stock quotes because that way they would "be spared the mental anguish caused him by other persons' mistakes of judgment."[5] What did he mean by "other persons' mistakes in judgment"? Well, here he is articulating the profound idea that has become the basis of all intelligent investing: *quoted market prices are but one opinion of value.*

This is not a new idea. A man name John Burr Williams wrote a hefty tome called *The Theory of Investment Value* back in 1930. In this book, Williams wrote eloquently about stock quotes being merely opinions of value set at the margin. Let's hear from Williams himself:

> Concerning its true worth, every man will cherish his own opinion; as to what price really is right, only time will tell. . . . [T]he market can only be an expression of opinion not a statement of fact. Today's opinion will mark today's price; tomorrow's opinion tomorrow's price; and seldom if ever will any price be exactly right as proved by the event.[6]

After laying out how stock market prices are opinions of value, Williams rolls into the dynamics of explaining the power of the *marginal opinion*:

> Both wise men and foolish will trade in the market, but no one group by itself will set the price. Nor will it matter what the majority, however overwhelming, may think; for the last owner, and he alone, will set the price. Thus the *marginal* opinion will determine the market price.[7]

Think of it this way: You live in a neighborhood of 300 homes where everyone thinks the value of a house there should be $400,000— except one guy, who sells his for $375,000. He is the marginal opinion. So guess what price gets recorded in the real estate transactions page of the local paper? Do you panic and sell your house because the guy down the street sold his for less? Of course not. You have your own feeling for the value of your home and your neighborhood.

This is a highly simplified example, of course, but markets are like this. The marginal buyers and sellers set prices. And marginal buyers and sellers enter into transactions for all sorts of reasons, not all of them good or even rational.

Stock prices can rise even though the underlying business is getting weaker. And stock prices can fall even though the underlying business is getting stronger.

As Seth Klarman—president of Baupost Group and another great investor we'll hear more from in these pages—notes, "It is vitally important for investors to distinguish stock price fluctuations from underlying business reality. If the general tendency is for buying to beget more buying and selling to precipitate more selling, investors must fight the tendency to capitulate to market forces."[8]

In other words, don't let market prices dictate your actions. It's for this reason that I oppose the use of stop-losses—investors mechanically selling a stock because it has fallen some prescribed amount. For example, some investors automatically sell out when a stock falls 25 percent. Bad idea in my view. (We'll be tackling the subject of when to sell in a later chapter. Having a good sell discipline is very important, and I've devoted an entire chapter to the topic). "Value in relation to price," Klarman continues, "and not price alone, must determine your investment decisions."[9]

The takeaway here is the importance of viewing market prices as the settled transactions of marginal buyers and sellers. That's all they are. They represent opinions of value at one point in time.

Put in this light, there is no reason to be worshipful of stock market quotes. They are simply prices to be taken advantage of or ignored, as the case may be. This is what the old master Benjamin Graham meant when he said the average investor would be better off without constant stock quotes—because the average investor makes too much of these prices.

This is not to say that you don't need to care about risk. The approach in this book is highly sensitized to risk. But the safety of an investment is measured in ways other than looking at the stock price.

Sound strange? Just hang in there and we'll get into a discussion of this measure of safety in the very next chapter. I assure you that after reading it, you'll think about safety and risk differently from now on.

These few points are important elements of my approach to investing. We'll talk about others in the rest of the book.

WHAT'S LESS IMPORTANT TO YOU AS A CONTROL INVESTOR?

If you're thinking like a dealmaker, notice the things that have now become less important to you.

(*Warning:* These next points might be shocking, offensive even. So have a seat, grab a nice drink, and try to relax. It all fits as part of the whole, but sometimes we have to clear away some of the brush before we can grow something new.)

You Don't Care about "Technical Factors"

That is, you're not really interested in "what the charts say." I can tell you from over a decade of making business deals as a corporate banker and over a decade as a financial writer that dealmakers don't consult stock charts. In my personal observation, no one thinks about charts except people who have come into the market first as traders. I can think of no business sale or transaction I've ever done or seen that involved people trying to determine when they would buy (or sell) by consulting a chart.

Put another way, you're more likely to think the charts hold some answers for you if you've never negotiated a business deal, never had to sell assets to raise money, or never managed a portfolio of businesses.

But chart readers don't see the tether that connects stock prices to the real world of flesh and blood and sweat and toil. They don't see the two markets—they only see the one. The quoted market prices are all-important to them; they take their cues from the action they see.

This is important, and unfortunately for many readers, this will be the hardest hurdle to get over because we see charts and chart readers everywhere. They are on the Internet, on the radio, and in magazines and newspapers. They sell books and speak at conferences and have great promotional copy telling you how you can turn a little money into a lot by watching Japanese candlestick patterns or other such tricks and patterns.

For these traders, charts are great. They can have a seemingly intelligent opinion on just about any stock just by running through some of their favorite charts. These people are speculators. They are short-term in-and-out traders. They are playing a whole other game than the people you will read about in this book. The approach I'm encouraging you to adopt is entirely different in its thinking and its foundations.

I'm not going to spend any time refuting chart reading. Some people use charts and fit them into an overall trading scheme, and that's fine. (Hey, some of my best friends are traders!) It's just not what this book is about.

So, in the words of the great Raymond Chandler's fictional detective Philip Marlowe, "Do I have to be polite? Or can I just be natural?" The hard-boiled, perhaps even rude, advice I have for you is this: Forget the charts.

You Don't Care as Much about the Big Picture

Most typical OPM investors love the big picture. They are very interested in what people think about where the economy is going, or what interest rates are going to do, or what the price of oil is going to be, among a myriad of other macro variables.

This is often called the top-down approach: an investor tries to think about the big picture (Are we entering a recession? Will consumer spending rise?) and then draw conclusions from that (U.S. stocks should rise; retailers should do well). They start at the top and work their way down until they find investments that fit with their big-picture view.

Relying on this kind of analysis is fraught with risk. You have to get many parts right for it to work consistently well. The investment approach in this book has fewer moving parts and a built-in margin of safety that is simply missing from the big-picture approach.

Klarman says it best:

> There is no margin of safety in top-down investing. The top-down investors are not buying based on value; they are buying based on a concept, theme or trend. There is no definable limit to the price they should pay, since value is not part of their purchase decision.[10]

The type of investing advocated here is a bottom-up strategy. The distinction is really one of emphasis. I write about big-picture stuff quite often, but when it comes to committing hard-earned money to an investment idea, I'm far more interested in the nitty-gritty details of the situation at hand.

The bottom-up investor understands and assesses value. He does this primarily by looking at the specifics of the investment under consideration. These specifics take precedence over his view of the economy at large. They trump his views on the market. He simply buys when he has found adequate values and refrains from buying when he can't find any.

Again, here is Klarman:

> Paradoxically a bottom-up strategy is in many ways simpler to implement than a top-down one. While a top-down investor must make several accurate predictions in a row, a bottom-up investor is not in the forecasting business at all.[11]

The whole strategy, Klarman writes, can be summed up as simply "buy a bargain and wait." As long as you have the tools and skills to assess value, you should come out ahead in the end—regardless of where the market is going at any particular time.

Control investors don't care about what they or anyone thinks about where the economy or market is headed. They make their decisions based on real-world factors and values that they see and understand and that are sitting there right in front of them. They are more interested in understanding the business they are investing in than the big picture. They are not in the prediction business. The investment approach in *Capital & Crisis* and in this book follows their lead.

You Care Less about Factors Like Earnings per Share, Price Earnings Ratios, and Consensus Forecasts

Again, typical OPM investors seem to talk about earnings about 90 percent of the time. If the average investor knows anything about a stock beyond its price, it's probably the last earnings per share number. For this reason alone, you should want to look at other things.

The truth is that this is the most manipulated number in the whole constellation of numbers an investor could look at. But more importantly, earnings don't necessarily capture the most essential element of a business—which is whether or not it is making money.

It may sound strange, but it's true.

Let's take a simplified example to show how this happens. Say a company makes a sale of $1 million and a profit of $300,000 on that sale. For purposes of accounting, it books the $300,000 as earnings (as it should), even though the company has not collected any cash.

This is common in business. You make a sale like that and you give terms. Maybe you get paid in ten days, which is great, but there is still a window during which you've booked a sale and profits and haven't collected any cash. Now, multiply this by the millions of sales the company makes in a year.

A business will always have an amount piled up in "money to be collected." This is called accounts receivable, and you can easily find it on a company's balance sheet.

In my banking career, we were acutely aware of the difference between earnings and cash flow. We had a saying: "Earnings don't repay loans—cash flow does." It was a reminder to always look beyond earnings and figure out the cash flow—the cycle of collections and disbursements. At times those cycles can vary widely; in fact, a company that otherwise appears profitable can suddenly find itself in a cash crunch.

Worse, you could end up like Lucent Technologies. Lucent made lots of sales and gave generous terms so it could keep booking those profits for Wall Street's benefit. It kept meeting earnings targets and showing nice growth, but meanwhile its accounts receivable were ballooning. Lucent wasn't collecting the cash nearly so well as it was booking sales!

So what happens? At some point you have to write off the uncollectible receivables. Lucent's customers started to get in trouble themselves and stopped paying their bills. Some went out of business entirely. All those pretty earnings had to be reversed out. That means the company reported losses. Suddenly, those earnings per share targets went out the window. The market took down the stock. It went from over $80 to under $5.

All it would have taken was a small effort to pay attention to Lucent's cash flows rather than its earnings, and you would have been out of that stock well before the rest of the market even knew what was going on.

That is why you pay attention to cash flow.

But paying attention to cash flow is more than just a protective measure—it's also a way to find real gems. We'll go into more detail about this part of the equation later in the book.

The consensus earnings estimates are something else investors seem to hang on with bated breath. I would urge you not to participate in the guessing game of trying to play on quarterly earnings numbers. If you follow the approach in this book, you won't worry about the quarterly numbers. You can relax a little bit more, go out and enjoy the day, and worry a lot less in general. Trust me, you will. You'll be more confident in what you own and why you own it and about what it's worth, and you won't care who knows it.

You Care Less about Dividends

Another shocker. There are a group of investors out there who, after asking about the price and price-earnings ratio, ask what the dividend yield is. If you to want think like a dealmaker, this is how you think about dividends: Dividends are a way for a company to pay shareholders some of the cash it has earned in its business. Dividend yield is just another factor in the analysis, and one to which a dealmaker gives no special weight.

The key question is this: How well is management allocating its resources? A company that borrows money to meet its dividend payment is probably not making a wise decision. Dividends are best paid with surplus cash flow that the business cannot put to good economic use.

So here is the assessment that needs to be made. Is management reinvesting in good projects or in a good business that is likely to create more cash for shareholders and for the business in the future? In other words, are they coming to decisions that make good use of precious resources?

One thing investors have to keep in mind is that management teams attain their position because of expertise—usually in their chosen industry. As Louis Lowenstein points out in his book *Sense and Nonsense in Corporate Finance*:

> The fact that a management team has one set of skills does not mean that it also has others or that it is wise to pay a substantial premium over market, as it must usually do, to acquire a business that, if the same funds were distributed, the shareholders could purchase on their own.[12]

Said differently, great managers are not necessarily *also* great investors. Sometimes you find companies with great managers and great investors. They are rare and usually worth hanging on to. One example would be Bruce Flatt at Brookfield Asset Management (formerly Brascan). I admire what Flatt has done with Brookfield, and I feel that his company is like a Berkshire Hathaway. You can hang on to it for a long time.

BROOKFIELD, BRUCE FLATT AND THE BRAZIL-CANADA CONNECTION

The old Brascan had roots stretching back to 1899, when it was engaged in the electric power and transit business in Brazil. It was started by entrepreneurial American and Canadian engineers and investors intrigued by the potential for railway and hydroelectric profits in that country of perpetual promise—Brazil.

Its operations, in Sao Paulo and Rio de Janeiro, were combined in 1912 to form the Brazilian Traction, Light, and Power Company. Though all the

(continues)

**BROOKFIELD, BRUCE FLATT AND THE
BRAZIL-CANADA CONNECTION (continued)**

action was in Brazil, the headquarters were on King Street in Toronto.
Known simply as "the Light," it grew to occupy a prominent place in
Brazilian business life. The Light would earn gobs of money and cruise
through six decades of Brazilian politics unscathed.

Dubbed "the Canadian Octopus" for its many interests in Brazil, the
outfit employed almost 50,000 people in the 1940s and supplied electricity,
water, transit, and telephone services to a sprawling network of customers.

However, a series of populist political movements in the 1960s seeking
to nationalize the country's industries soured the business environment in
Brazil, turning profits into losses. After years of negotiation, the company
sold parts of the business to the Brazilian government.

With the proceeds (due in installments over a period of years), the company made its first Canadian investment, buying shares of Labatt Brewery.
It was the first of many. The name was changed to Brascan in 1969 (by
combining the first syllables of Brazil and Canada) to better reflect the
growing emphasis on Canadian investments while still retaining a link
to its unique heritage. Even now, the company has hydroelectric power
plants and other real estate in Brazil.

By the 1980s, Brascan had grown into an unwieldy conglomerate
of widely disparate businesses that seemed to be involved in nearly
everything—beer, insurance, metals, oil, financial services, forestry products, and more. Its complex financial structure mirrored its scattershot
portfolio of businesses, and its balance sheet was laden with mounds of
debt. At its peak, the company represented nearly one-third of the entire
market capitalization of the Toronto Stock Exchange.

Brascan was a bit late to the conglomerate party, which was a hot
investment idea in the 1960s. Investment writer John Train called the
boom in conglomerates "one of the most elaborate and most expensive
(countless billions of dollars) deceptions ever perpetrated on investors."[13]

The idea of a conglomerate is based on several flimsy theories.
Among them is the idea that you can buy lots of businesses using debt
and show great gains in earnings with each new acquisition (via the
magic of accounting, often called "cooking the books"). The problem
with this theory, of course, is that it resembles a Ponzi scheme.

Eventually, you just have too much debt when the hard times inevitably come. Then you are sunk.

Another problem then, among many, was the idea that you could find a management team that could skillfully manage, for example, a beer business, an insurance company, a metal miner, and a restaurant chain—all at once. When the conglomerates fell apart in the late 1960s, investors lost a bundle and quickly came to distrust conglomerates as profitable investments, though there were notable exceptions (such as General Electric). Investors, though, forget, or perhaps they just don't read history.

While Brascan was following the blueprint of these dead conglomerates from the 1960s, investors seemed to think this story would end differently. Maybe Brascan's management team would be one of the exceptions and play the game better than its financial forebears. But management, however skilled, can't beat back debt without cash.

The Transformation of an Ugly Conglomerate

The enormous debts the company piled up in building its sprawling empire did the company no favors during the real estate collapse in the early 1990s, which brought Brascan under the heels of its creditors. Brascan had to sell off assets quickly to raise cash and survive—not the best way to get value for what you are selling. Though the company narrowly avoided collapse, investors were badly burned in the process, and Brascan shares fell out of favor.

So in the mid-1990s began the long rehabilitation project, which prominently featured a sort of decade-long yard sale designed to slim down and simplify the overwrought empire. These actions achieved much more than that, *as the company today is totally transformed.* Gone are the beer business, the insurance business, the oil companies, and a host of other noncore and underperforming investments.

The man behind much of this transformation has been Bruce Flatt, who took the top job at Brascan in 2002, completing a turnaround his predecessor began. Flatt's vision for Brascan, which he repeats often, is one of a simple company running office buildings and generating power. With billions of dollars in proceeds from these kinds of sales, the company has reinvested much of it in prime real estate and power plants. It still sits on a mountain of cash.

(continues)

**BROOKFIELD, BRUCE FLATT AND THE
BRAZIL-CANADA CONNECTION** *(continued)*

The folks at Brascan like to refer to their company as an asset management company. It's not hard to see why, since the company owns a variety
of assets, some of which seem not to have much to do with one another.
However, there is a grand plan here, a neat logic interlocking the company
and its future direction.

Flatt, before taking the top job at Brascan, was president of Brookfield
Homes and led its transformation from a hodgepodge collection of indus-
trial, retail, and office properties into a glimmering portfolio of class A
office properties in leading cities, including Manhattan's World Financial
Center (which was damaged in the September 11 attacks), Toronto's BCE
Place, and Calgary's Bankers Hall.

Given Flatt and his team's track record so far, I wouldn't want to bet
against them. In fact, Flatt and many of his senior executives are also shareholders in about 17 percent of the company. They refer to themselves as
partners and work in open spaces, as opposed to individual offices. One of
Flatt's heroes is Warren Buffett. Indeed, he has several Buffett-like qualities—
he still drives around in a 1996 Ford Explorer and has a reputation for being
something of a miser. He thinks long-term ("We're running this place looking out a decade or more," he says) and personally owns 4.7 million shares,
worth over $160 million. ("I've never sold a share," he says.)

But the most Buffett-like thing about him may be his investment performance. Since Flatt became CEO three years ago, the average annual
return to shareholders (including dividends) is nearly 30 percent.

———

This piece was originally published in the March 2005 issue of *Capital
& Crisis*.[14] As I write, Brookfield Asset Management is still a core part of
the *C&C* portfolio and a solid long-term holding. But the point here is that
Flatt appears to be a solid manager *and* a good allocator of capital. He
thinks like a good investor ought to.

THE CONCEPT OF OPPORTUNITY COST

The concept of *opportunity cost* simply means that by doing one thing, you forgo the opportunity to do another thing. When you play golf one afternoon instead of staying home and watching the football game, your opportunity cost is the football game. You are going to miss it and play golf instead. You have only so much time. Corporate managers have to make these kinds of decisions all the time with the limited amount of resources they command. They have to decide which actions to pursue and which to forgo. The dividend policy process ought to be part of that thinking.

The bottom line here is that we are not looking for businesses that pay high dividends today. We may find a good investment opportunity that also pays a high dividend, but we are not actively seeking high dividend payers. There is a difference there I hope you will see.

WHAT COMPANIES DO WITH THEIR CASH

Charlie Munger likes to use a schematic that includes no-brainers, gold mines, cash cows, and cash traps. A *no-brainer* is an investment you must make if you are to have any chance at success. This kind of investment includes the usually basic investments you must make to keep your business running smoothly. The losses from not making these investments would be too much to take. The *gold mines* are investments that are expected to produce substantial returns for a long period of time. A *cash cow* requires some minimal investment to keep the cash coming, but in this investment you expect the cash eventually to peter out. And finally, *cash traps* are those investments that require lots of investment but throw off less than they required. Cash traps are the kinds of investments we don't want to see our companies making.

Many companies hesitate to pay a dividend because they see it as some sort of admission of failure. They see paying a dividend as telling the market, "Our business has no good investment opportunities with its cash, and the best we can come up with is to pay a dividend." It may be okay for a while to just let the cash pile up—but doing so is likely to make such a company the target of activists. You should avoid management teams that routinely splurge on pricey acquisitions.

Deciding what's what is not always easy or clear-cut. But these are the kinds of ideas we keep in mind in thinking about how a company uses its money.

Ultimately, we want to get money out of the investments we make. You would never invest in any shares if you did not expect that at some point you and the other shareholders were going to get a piece of the money earned.

BUY WHOLESALE, SELL RETAIL

Here are a few real-world examples to help you understand the two-market proposition in action.

It's about playing Wall Street against Main Street, as rarely do they agree about the price of anything. Sometimes Wall Street values certain assets above what private investors would pay. At other times Wall Street prices out-of-favor assets well below what private investors would pay.

Whenever I discover assets in the stock market that are selling for deep discounts on their real-world values, I have usually discovered a compelling investment opportunity . . . as I did in October 2004.

Back then the stock market was assigning an insultingly low valuation to the shares of Orient-Express Hotels (NYSE: OEH), an owner and operator of luxury hotels, restaurants, and tourist trains. By buying OEH stock, you were paying far less for comparable hotel assets than what private market buyers were paying for similar properties. Not only that, but hotel properties of all types had been commanding ever-higher prices in 2003 and 2004. The average price per room for luxury hotels in 2004 was about $140,000 and climbing (see Figure 1.1).

Super-luxury hotels of the sort that Orient-Express owns were commanding a multiple of that price. Orient's Hotel Cipriani in Venice, for instance, is one of the world's finest hotels—fitted with precious marble and stucco. Room rates were as high as $5,000 per night, and industry experts estimated that the 103-room hotel was worth at least $1 million per room. That was just one asset in OEH's portfolio.

Looking at transactions for super-luxury hotels could give you a better sense of this market. The Four Seasons in Maui sold for an estimated $740,000 per room in 2004, for example. Yet the stock market was valuing Orient-Express at only $226,000 per room in 2004—not including the value of its interests in three fine restaurants and luxury trains.

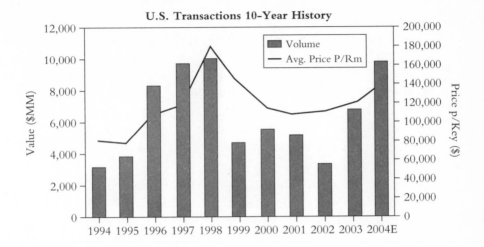

FIGURE 1.1   Ten-Year History of U.S. Transactions

Reprinted from Chris Mayer, "The World's Most Exclusive Hotels," *Capital & Crisis,* no. 8 (November 2004).

So I recommended the stock to my subscribers. After more than doubling in price over the ensuing 18 months, Orient-Express shares are no longer cheap. In fact, they look quite pricey indeed, which is why I urged my *Capital & Crisis* subscribers to book their profits and await the next opportunity.

When I sold it, Orient-Express traded at an EV-to-EBITDA ratio of nearly 25 times. The stock had gone up a lot, and now it was expensive. The value the stock market put on Orient-Express was nearly double what control investors paid for hotel assets at the time. For example, Hilton Hotels Corporation agreed to purchase the hotels of its European namesake for about 12 times the estimated 2006 EBITDA.

And many people thought that was high. I realize they are not truly comparable properties. Nonetheless, the gap is huge. This kind of analysis—taking a look at private transactions and the prices that control investors are paying—is extremely useful for figuring out what's cheap and what's not. *Most investors only compare publicly traded companies to other publicly traded companies—entirely neglecting this important "second" market for stocks where prices are determined by well-informed buyers and sellers.*

Another interesting example of the private-public market arbitrage involves Intrawest (NYSE: IDR), an owner and operator of ski resorts, including the highly prized Whistler Mountain operation. I recommended the stock in April 2005 when it was trading at an EV-to-EBITDA multiple of only 6 times. The private market was swapping comparable properties for 11 times and greater. For example, Intrawest sold its majority interest in the Mammoth Ski Resort to Starwood Capital for 11 times its EBITDA.

One year later the stock was up 80 percent since my initial recommendation—and a private equity firm, Fortress Capital, eventually bought the whole company.

I'll leave you with one other example. I recommended NewAlliance Bancshares (NYSE: NAL), a Connecticut-based thrift, in *Capital & Crisis*. The price-to-tangible book ratio—a commonly cited ratio when dealing with financial institutions—was only about 1.8 times for NewAlliance.

If you compile a list of recent transactions for thrifts and banks, you'll see that the acquisition multiple paid was closer to three times the tangible book. Table 1.1 shows the top deals in 2005, limited to banks in the New England and mid-Atlantic regions.

Table 1.1 is limited to deals of at least $100 million. Smaller transactions get smaller multiples. But even if you include all of them, the average price-to-tangible book ratio paid is about 2.5 times.

TABLE 1.1 2005 Deals with New England or Mid-Atlantic Target

Buyer/Target	Price/Tangible Book Announcement
Sovereign Bancorp. Inc./Independence Community Bank Corporation	3.46
TD Banknorth Inc./Hudson United Bancorp	4.46
New York Community Bancorp/ Atlantic Bank of New York	1.80
Fulton Financial Corporation/ Columbia Bancorp	3.24
Susquehanna Bancshares Inc./ Minotola National Bank	2.06
Willow Grove Bancorp Inc./ Chester Valley Bancorp Inc.	2.74
UCBH Holding Inc./ Great Eastern Bank	3.36

Data from SNL Financial.

NewAlliance is a substantial bank, the fifth-largest in Connecticut, which is a desirable and affluent market. Even if you use only the 2.5 times tangible book, you get a price of around $20 or $21. That's nearly 40 percent higher than the market price of $14.51 at the time. The bank is overcapitalized, which is one reason it has been buying back its stock and boosting its dividend.

This one we sold for a small profit. You may wonder, then, why would I include this example? Well, nothing works all the time. You should know that up front. The approach to investing I use produces a high batting average, but no one bats a thousand. What I aim to do is keep my mistakes small and my profits large. Over time I know I'll come out ahead.

All the stocks I've mentioned provide an opportunity to profit from the pricing disparities between public market values and private transaction values. So whenever you're trying to buy stocks cheap, you can't afford to ignore what's happening in the private markets. Whenever Wall Street and Main Street disagree, opportunities emerge.

POSTSCRIPT

To keep it simple, I'm sticking with the two-market schematic in this book. In the real world there are actually more than two markets. For example, there is the liquidation value of a company's assets. This is the value of a company if you sold it off in pieces.

A Third Market: Liquidation Value . . . and Benjamin Graham's "Net-Nets"

Benjamin Graham liked to look at stocks that were selling in the market for less than their liquidation value—in other words, stocks so cheap that if the company were shut down and sold, investors would still make money. Not a lot of businesses meet that criterion.

Graham called these stocks "bargain issues" or "net current asset stocks." Today we often call these stocks "net-nets." Graham thought that if an investor could limit himself to buying 30 such names, he ought to do real well.

In fact, it was so obvious to the great master that he seemed almost embarrassed to say so. "It always seemed, and still seems," Graham wrote, "ridiculously simple to say that if one can acquire a diversified group of common stocks selling for less than the applicable net current assets alone—after deducting all prior claims, and counting as *zero* the fixed and other assets . . . the results should be quite satisfactory."[15]

For more than 30 years, this simple formula served Graham well. The problem, however, is that net-nets are a rare fish. Even Graham admits that running his screen did not always produce many ideas. Running the net-net filter in 1968, for example, would have brought in "only a handful, at most, of such issues."[16]

Most of the net-nets were troubled companies that investors hated, and that was why they were trading where they were. That was also why Graham's "formula" was able to work. It went against human nature. People read his ideas, they understood them, but they couldn't follow them.

As with religion—we may understand the Ten Commandments, but there are just too many temptations—the vast majority of investors may understand a sensible approach but will not be able to stay on the righteous path.

Sometimes Graham's beloved net-nets required stoic patience on the part of the investor to make good on the cheap shares. In writing about them, Graham warned readers not to lose patience with them if they didn't immediately rise in price. "Sometimes the patience needed may appear quite considerable." He related his experience in holding a net-net for three and a half years and making 165 percent—a 47 percent annual return. But almost the entire gain occurred in the fourth year. "Most of the bargain issues in our experience have not taken so long to show good profits," Graham confided.[17] But the lesson is there.

Net-nets are all but extinct on today's major exchanges. After all, Graham hatched the idea in the 1920s and applied it during the Great Depression, when cheap stocks were rather plentiful. The world is different today.

In my banking career, this liquidation value could also be an important number. But for investors, given the kinds of businesses they look at, liquidation prices seldom come into play.

Still, while true net-nets are extremely rare in the current market environment, the idea is still sound. We'll take a look at a variation of Graham's approach to finding winning stocks in Chapter 4.

So, let's leave this digression and get back to the two-market model for stocks. Once you understand and buy into the idea, other investing concepts—like margin of safety—start to make a lot more sense.

CHAPTER 2

THE DEALMAKER'S TOOLBOX

The goal of this book is to help you think like a dealmaker. In this chapter, I'm going to give you some of the basic tools of the trade. One of the best ways to do that is to study the wizardry of deal-makers in years past. Another term for these dealmakers might be "money minds."

The money mind, as described by Phil Carret (founder of the Pioneer Fund and author of *The Art of Speculation* and *A Money Mind at Ninety*), involves "an instinctive reaction to any bit of information that comes to one's attention: How, if at all, can one profit by it?"[1]

The story of John Patterson is the story of one such money mind in action.

Patterson, a small retail merchant struggling to make a buck in 1880s America, installed a new, crude device that basically performed the functions of a cash register. Patterson noticed an instant improvement in the financial performance of his store. The reason? It became much harder for his employees to steal.

Patterson, though, did not contentedly sit back and congratulate himself on how this marvelous machine had saved his struggling retail business. No, Patterson decided to go into the cash register business. In 1884 National Cash Register was born.

Charlie Munger, vice chairman of Berkshire Hathaway, related this story in his famous speech on worldly wisdom. Munger observed, "A well-educated orangutan could see that buying into partnership with

Patterson in those early days, given his notions about the cash register business, was a total, 100 percent cinch."[2]

Investors, Munger advises, should be on the lookout for these kinds of situations. Though an investor may come across only a handful of them in a lifetime, they can make all the difference.

Perhaps Munger overstates his case by saying NCR was "a total, 100 percent cinch." Nothing in the affairs of human beings, of which the stock market is a part, is ever that certain it seems to me. Usually, there are far more things that can go wrong than things that will go right. Success comes from repeatedly making good risk-reward decisions: betting when the odds favor you, and holding back when they do not.

When many forces are working in your favor, amplifying and reinforcing each other, you get what Munger calls a "lollapalooza effect." Forces combine, and the result is more than simple addition. As Munger says, "It's often like a critical mass in physics, where you get a nuclear explosion if you get to a certain point of mass—and you don't get anything much worth seeing if you don't reach the mass."[3]

NCR later introduced the first electric cash register. Today NCR is a business on the NYSE with a $6 billion market cap and is engaged in all kinds of information technology services. That's the power of a lollapalooza effect.

And it all started with Patterson's vision and his knack for seeing a profit opportunity—the essence of a money mind.

Before we get too far along, I have to spend some time introducing you to important tools. This chapter is undoubtedly the most difficult in the book. But give it a try, and I promise things will get better. I'm going to keep this simple so that you get the gist of the ideas. Don't panic if you think you won't be able to use these insights right away— we'll flesh them out later in the book. *There are three big ideas here that will change your assumptions about investing.* And believe me, the money minds know these ideas.

Before we get into the details, I want to preface this section with a few comments about numbers in general. Some investors obsess over numbers. Over the years I've found that understanding what the numbers are is less important than understanding what they mean. In other words, you're better off focusing on *why* the number is what it is— drawing the connection to the real world.

All financial numbers relate to each other in many ways. Companies with high profit margins tend to have high returns on equity. Companies with a lot of debt tend to trade for lower price-to-book ratios. These are just a couple of examples. Don't worry if you don't understand some of these terms. We'll get to them. But if you understand that numbers are related, you will be less likely to fall in love with companies that put up some kind of gaudy numbers and more likely to spend time thinking about why they did that and how their numbers relate to other numbers and concepts.

So the emphasis in this section is on concepts, not the deception that precise numbers can create. Again, we want to know what the numbers mean and not so much what they are. I've also found that being mostly right is more important than getting things exactly right. It's more important to be in the right neighborhood.

THINK ABOUT THE WHOLE BUSINESS, NOT JUST THE STOCK PRICE

The first important concept is to always think about the whole business, not just the stock price.

The average investor typically thinks about the price of his stock in terms of its quoted stock price, as I've noted. But even then, the investor often misunderstands what that stock price represents. The quoted price is just the price of equity—it doesn't take into account, for example, the price of any debts.

Think of when you buy a house. You don't ask, "What's the value of the equity in the house?" Nobody cares about that. You want to make an offer based on what you think the house is worth and on what you are willing to pay. Normally, the seller will take the proceeds, pay off his mortgage completely, and keep the rest (after expenses).

So the price of the house has two components: the value of the equity and the value of the debt. You pay off the debt first. Equity is the residual. It's the same with companies. You have two components: equity and debt. The quoted stock price is only the equity component.

You can take the quoted stock price and translate that into an equity value for the whole business. If the stock price is $25 per share, and the total number of shares out there (or outstanding, as we say) is 10 million, then the value of the equity in the market is $250 million.

Let's say the business has a $300 million mortgage. If you're buying the stock, you'd probably like to know that, wouldn't you? You'd want to factor that in. So when you see that the company made a profit of $40 million, you want to compare that to the value of the equity *and the debt*. A profit of $40 million may look cheap on an equity value of $250 million. It looks different against a value of $550 million (the $250 million plus the $300 million in debt). The $550 million is the value of the *whole* business.

Okay, now you're halfway to understanding the concept of enterprise value, which you can think of as a theoretical price to pay for the *entire* company—equity plus debt.

But there's another component we have to think about: excess or surplus cash. Again, let's consider the example of buying a house. You have two houses to choose from. Each is selling for $500,000, but one house has a drawer stuffed with $200,000 in cash—and the drawer and its contents "convey," that is, you get to keep it.

You'd want to know which house that was, wouldn't you? And all things being equal, you'd prefer the house with money stuffed in it.

It's the same with investing, and it's the same way in thinking about these companies. Sometimes you will find companies that are stuffed with cash. If you pay $25 per share, the cash works out to $5 to $10 or more per share. That's a significant source of value that most investors never consider.

Excess cash in effect lowers the price you pay for the company. If you buy the house with the cash, for example, then your purchase price is really only $300,000 ($500,000 less the $200,000 cash you get right back). It's the same with companies. If you pay $15 per share for a stock, and it has $5 per share in cash, then your real price, for purposes of valuing the business, is only $10 per share.

If that company earned $1 per share in profits, you can safely say that it is trading for a multiple of 10 times earnings, as opposed to 15. The stock is cheaper than it first appears.

Of course, analyzing cash takes more than just looking at the cash itself. If the company is not profitable and instead is burning through its cash, then you have to factor that in. But if the company is healthy and profitable and even adding to its cash pile over time—well, that's something to look at. My experience has been that these are good companies to own, because that cash gives the company a lot of options to add value to the business (and thus to your shares). There's more on the ways to create wealth in the next chapter.

Now you have the elements to calculate enterprise value (EV): market cap plus debt minus cash. This is an important tool, and it will be the basic thing you use to compare different firms and investments. Again, we think about enterprise value because we think in terms of *whole* companies. (If you want to cheat, some websites like Yahoo Finance! have enterprise values calculated for you. Just click on key statistics and you'll see it there.)

Now that we have a company's EV, what do we do with it? Primarily, we compare it with other numbers, like cash flow. Let's look at that next.

THINK ABOUT CASH FLOW, NOT EARNINGS

Smash, dough, fiddlies, coin, tin, silver, hay, oot, shekels, ice, mazooma, bread, sponduliks, silver—cash has been known by many names over the years. No matter what you call it, cash is the second important concept to think about when you're investing: cash flow, not just earnings.

The essential reason every investor ought to think about cash flows and not earnings is that the two can diverge significantly. And cash flow is by the far the more important of the two. A company simply cannot survive without cash flow over the long haul. Remember the example I gave you in the last chapter—Lucent booked sales and profits even though it hadn't collected the cash.

One simple reason we follow cash flow rather than earnings is for defensive purposes. A company may be reporting nice earnings even though it is not translating those earnings into real cash. That's a very important reason why following the cash will keep you out of some impending disasters.

Doing that, however, is not as simple as just investing in companies that are generating lots of cash flow. Rapidly growing companies may show nice earnings and poor cash flows for years. And they may still be worth investing in. Nevertheless, the approach in this book emphasizes cash flows. So, typically, a company that consumes a lot of cash is not likely to be a candidate for investment in our approach.

There is another reason to follow cash flows other than just playing defense and avoiding losers. Cash flows can alert you to some real gems that the market is entirely overlooking.

So what is cash flow specifically?

One basic proxy for cash flow is to add noncash charges like depreciation to earnings, then take out capital expenditures. That's one decent and rough measure of cash flow—though it does not include working capital changes.

Working capital changes include things like changes in inventory and accounts receivable. Such factors can have an impact on cash flow, and it pays to consider them when looking at a company.

When inventory rises, that logically reflects a use of cash. A company with increasing amounts of inventory is tying up money in that inventory. The same with accounts receivable. Accounts receivable is simply money owed to the company for services rendered or product delivered. Higher amounts of accounts receivable tie up cash.

Now, companies don't have to use only their own cash to fund these things. They have vendors that give them terms. Let's say your inventory is lumber, and you've gotten 30-day terms from Lumber Supply. You don't absorb the whole cost of all the lumber in your inventory: you finance pieces of it. This financing shows on financial statements as accounts payable.

When we take accounts receivable and inventory and subtract accounts payable, we get a number called working capital.

Working capital changes are important and real, and as mentioned earlier, they have an impact on cash flow. Rising working capital requirements absorb cash. You can find all of these numbers on the balance sheet.

Expect these numbers to grow over time with sales and earnings. Inventory and accounts receivable rising faster than sales could be a warning sign. Old inventory may be piling up, or the company may have sloppy inventory controls. Accounts receivable may be rising because the company is booking sales by giving easy terms but finding it more difficult to convert those sales to cash.

These are issues to think about. There are no easy ways to sort them out, and no pat numbers to use. You have to make comparisons to other companies in the same industry and try to understand what is going on in the business. There may be perfectly legitimate reasons for the patterns in a company's cash flow; you just have to find them out.

Are you disappointed by this conclusion? Perhaps you're reading this and saying, "Well, this is all well and good, but I can't use this. I don't know what to do or how to start. . . ."

Unfortunately, there are no easy answers. You'll just have to get used to looking at financial statements—income statements, balance sheets, and cash flows. And maybe more importantly, you'll have to get used to asking and thinking about these questions.

As an investor, you hold all the cards. If a company's finances are too hard to understand and you're not sure what to do to understand them better, then you can pass and look for another company. I tell my readers often: Never feel rushed to invest. The stock market will be here tomorrow and the day after, and for a long time after that.

Anyway, you can use the basic proxy of net income plus noncash items (depreciation and amortization) less capital expenditures with the previous comments in mind. What are capital expenditures? They are investments the company makes in its own business. Capital expenditures are often disclosed in press releases. In financial statements, you'll find the number in the statement of cash flows, under investing activities, usually called something like "capital expenditures" or "addition to fixed investments."

This number has two components; neither is usually disclosed, but both are worth considering. The first component is ongoing maintenance. Every company has to plow a certain amount of money back into the business. The second component is funding for growth or expansion. The considerable amount of money that some companies spend on expansion efforts can make their cash flow numbers look worse than they are. That's because money invested for expansion is obviously discretionary. That is, management didn't have to spend it, but they chose to, perhaps for very good reasons.

Some investors have a bias against companies or businesses that require high levels of capital expenditures and don't want to own "capital-intensive" businesses. I think this bias is not wise. What is more important is whether the business is making—or is reasonably likely to make—a good return on its investments.

Plus, the overlooked aspect of a capital-intensive business is that the high level of capital expenditures required can be a deterrent against new competition, which has to invest so much to get started.

A frequent modification made to the cash flow calculation is to also add back interest expense and taxes. Then you get the infamous EBITDA: earnings before interest, taxes, depreciation, and amortization. I say "infamous" because during the bubble years of the late nineties many companies and analysts abused this ratio and started to focus on it to the exclusion of the other real factors that I've already mentioned—things like capital expenditures and working capital.

So EBITDA got a bad name. But as long as you understand its limitations, it is useful in comparing companies and looking for bargains.

Why, you may wonder, do you add back interest expense when calculating EBIDTA? Well, you add back interest expense because you are going to use it to compare firms based on enterprise value. Remember, in the EV calculation you've included net debt. Some firms have debt and some don't. If you don't also add back interest expense to get EBITDA, you'll get a distorted view. You have to add back interest expense to earnings so that you are comparing apples to apples.

For the same reason, you add back taxes, primarily because debt levels have an impact on taxes, since interest is tax-deductible. By adding these two things back, you can reasonably compare different businesses in the same industry without allowing financing decisions—such as how much debt to carry—to color the basic profitability comparison.

The Dealmaker's Ratio

You can use enterprise value and compare it with EBTIDA to get a quick snapshot on value. I call this EV-to-EVITDA ratio *the dealmaker's ratio,* because dealmakers often target companies with low EV-to-EBITDA ratios. Some brokerage houses will even run EV-to-EBITDA screens when trolling around for buyout candidates.

Low numbers are good—with caveats. Again, we want to understand what they mean, not necessarily what they are. A low EV-to-EBITDA may just mean that the market expects earnings to go in the tank. A high EV-to-EBITDA ratio may mean that the company is cyclical, earnings were unusually low, and now the market expects a dramatic increase.

So that's your primer on cash flow. Now you're thinking about whole companies, not just the equity piece. And you're thinking about cash flows, not just about earnings.

Let's move on to the third vital piece of the analytical tool kit: assets and financial strength.

A HIDDEN BUT VITAL INFRASTRUCTURE

AVX Corporation (NYSE: AVX) makes electrical components of all kinds. These parts regulate, filter, and store electrical energy. Essentially, they are the hidden infrastructure inside nearly every electronic device—the crucial components behind cell phones, radios, computers, and much more. Anything that needs electrical components could be a potential user of AVX's broad and diverse product line, which covers over 100,000 product types.

For example, AVX makes 90 percent of the components found in a laptop computer (which has over 1,800 components). It also provides 85 percent of the parts used in a typical cell phone (which has over 500 parts). Just think of all the electronics used by a modern automobile—AVX makes components for those, too. The range of AVX products and applications is staggering.

And with new services and innovations driving the demand for electronic parts, there is no end in sight to the growing number and complexity of these components.

In terms of increasing complexity, just look at the circuit board of the original Intel Pentium processor. That chip had 252 components. Today's Pentium uses over 900 components. Let me give you another example: Electronic content in automobiles grew from 35 percent of the vehicle's cost in 2004 to 41 percent in 2005. Electronics in automobiles will be almost 50 percent of vehicle cost by 2006.

I think you'll agree that the demand for electrical components is not likely to go away anytime soon. If anything, electronic devices will only get more complicated and more varied—creating a further need for newer and more specialized components.

A Cyclical Business with a Tremendous Upside

Despite that rosy picture, very few electronics companies manage to produce consistent profits. The industry goes through periods of

(continues)

A HIDDEN BUT VITAL INFRASTRUCTURE *(continued)*

boom followed by periods of bust—too much supply, falling prices, and falling profits. Recent years have been most accurately described as bust.

You can see how AVX's sales and profits surged in the period from 1999 to 2001. After the peak in 2001, the company's results basically flatlined. In the 2002–2004 period, the company reported small losses (though it remained cash flow–positive; more on that later). Then, in 2005, AVX reported increasing sales and profits for the first time in years. In looking at Table 2.1, 2005 looks a lot like 1999—and that's good news.

TABLE 2.1   Free Cash Flow Even During Rough Times

	2002	2003	2004	2005
Cash from operating activities	302.2	122.4	83.5	57.1
Capital expenditures	(75.5)	(38.3)	(33.7)	(48.3)
Free cash flow	226.7	84.1	49.8	8.8

This was exactly the time to consider buying a company like AVX. The trough was behind it, and the upside remained. When times are good in this industry, they can be very good. At the peak, the company earned over $3 per share. If you slap a price-earnings ratio of only 10 times on that number, you get $30 per share—more than double the $12 share price at the time.

Still, those were crazy times. We don't need a return to the 2000 bubble to make good on this investment. AVX routinely generated well over $1 per share in cash flow and reliably cranked out steady free cash flow for several years prior to 2000.

And to AVX's credit, it generated positive free cash flow even in the industry's worst years.

In short, AVX is a proven survivor, a resilient competitor in a tough industry.

AVX, however, is clearly operating well below its potential. It has a hidden unappreciated ability to deliver much higher levels of future cash flow.

The Olstein Financial Alert Fund is a respected value shop that practices the art of picking up companies operating at less than their full potential. In fact, this practice has been a critical part of its invest-ment success. I've had successes, too, buying companies with cyclically depressed earnings.

Eric Heyman, director of research for Olstein, wrote recently about this aspect of Olstein's approach. "When a company's potential is not readily apparent, it tends to sell at a material discount to private market value," he noted. "Most investors only react to what can be easily seen and don't undertake further analysis . . . by the time the investment masses identify the changes in the company, the valuation gap is usually closed in rapid fashion."[4]

In other words, by the time the masses get wind of the positive changes at AVX, the stock price should rise quickly.

Not surprisingly, Olstein owns a $20 million stake in AVX, making it one of the largest institutional investors in AVX. The team at Third Avenue, like-minded tangible asset investors, is the largest institutional investor in AVX, with a $98 million investment—more than 5 percent of the company. Both Olstein and Third Avenue have returned more than double the S&P 500 over the past 10 years.

It's always good to know I'm in such smart company. Then, too, there was that balance sheet. . . .

I love companies with pristine balance sheets. They are ready for any-thing this wild world can throw at them. Plus, cash can be a catalyst for good things to happen—like share buybacks and dividends—not to men-tion that it gives the company the means to make investments to improve the business.

With $725 million in cash and liquid assets and no debt, AVX fits my profile perfectly. That's about $4.19 per share in cash assets. Backing all that out of the $12 stock price leaves you paying about $8 for the rest of the business. And keep in mind that this is a business that has the potential to crank out at least a buck per share in cash flow when things are more normal—and a lot more if things get really good.

The median price-to-book ratio over the last 10 years was 2.1. AVX was trading for only 1.5 times book. Just to get to the median, the stock would have to rise 40 percent.

I recommended AVX in October 2005. By April 2006, it had gained over 60 percent.

THINK ABOUT ASSET VALUES

It would be a mistake to think that all the facts that describe a particular investment are or could be known. Not only may questions remain unanswered; all the right questions may not even have been asked. Even if the present could somehow be perfectly understood, most investments are dependent on outcomes that cannot be accurately foreseen.[5]

—*Seth Klarman*

Klarman describes it well. There is a lot of uncertainty investors must deal with in every investment. You can never know all there is to know. And you can and will make mistakes. For these reasons, I love Graham's concept of a *margin of safety.*

The margin of safety concept is the idea that you want to buy an investment at a price that gives you room for uncertainties and errors. As Benjamin Graham David and Dodd say:

The safety sought in investment is not absolute or complete; the word means, rather, protection against loss under all normal or reasonably likely conditions or variations. . . . A safe stock is one which holds every prospect of being worth the price paid except under quite unlikely contingencies.[6]

Buffett describes the margin of safety this way: "When you build a bridge, you insist it can carry 30,000 pounds, but you only drive 10,000-pound trucks across it. And that same principle works in investing."[7]

The best way I've found to ensure some margin of safety in your investments is to think about asset values—indeed, a focus on buying tangible assets at a discount is a great way to lower risk and still enjoy sweet returns.

What are tangible assets? These are the things you can see, touch, and count—things like buildings and real estate, cash, barrels of oil, hydroelectric dams, water rights, timberlands, factories, and more. Perhaps it is easier to understand tangible assets by comparing them to intangible ones. Intangible assets are things like goodwill, development costs, and even licenses or brand names.

And what do I mean by buying tangible assets at a discount? By "discount" I'm referring again to the two-market model. We know the stock price in the publicly traded market. That is the market we are going to buy from or sell into, as the case may be. But we don't have to accept that price as an accurate statement of value. So in trying to figure out if we can buy at a discount, we have to try to break down our investments into pieces we can understand, compare these pieces to private market values, and therefore value the whole. I showed you a few examples in the last chapter.

In my newsletter, I've always expressed a preference for buying tangible assets, which is a great opportunity when you can find it. Buying tangible assets is a high-percentage play.

Let me again borrow from Klarman, who writes in his book:

> Tangible assets . . . are more precisely valued and therefore provide investors with greater protection from loss. Tangible assets usually have value in alternate uses, thereby providing a margin of safety. If a chain of retail stores becomes unprofitable, for example, the inventories can be liquidated, leases transferred, and real estate sold.[8]

Conversely, when it comes to buying a well-known soft-drink company like Dr. Pepper, you will probably wind up paying a high price relative to its underlying book value, because the market gives a lot of value to—or credit for—the Dr. Pepper brand. But, as Klarman says, "if consumers lose their taste for Dr. Pepper, by contrast, tangible assets will not meaningfully cushion investors' losses."[9]

Here he is emphasizing the role of tangible assets in creating a cushion to protect against adversity—again, a margin of safety. We'll see in the next chapter that buying companies with loads of tangible assets can also be a source of future wealth creation.

So how do we think about asset values?

The first proxy is simple book value, which, counter to its name, is not a value per se. This number is readily available and is simply a product of accounting conventions. Still, it is a good starting place from which you can make adjustments. You can find book value on most financial sites. Or you can look at a balance sheet and use the total stockholders' equity number. (If you prefer to think in terms of book value per share, you can just take the total stockholders' equity number and divide it by the total number of shares outstanding.)

The first adjustment I make is to strip out intangibles. I always work with a tangible book value—for the reasons we've just covered.

Once you have that, you can mark down any other assets you think are not worth much, or you can add value to assets that are not on the balance sheet or are not valued at current market prices.

The classic example is a company that bought real estate years ago and now is sitting on property that has doubled or tripled over that time: accounting convention requires that these assets be depreciated over time, or written off little by little every year. IRSA—the Argentine landholder I wrote about in Chapter 1—carried that big parcel of land on their books at $39 million. That was the price they had paid years before. The land was now worth probably 15 times that amount.

The essential idea is to go over a company's balance sheet, think about the company's assets, and try to put some values in those assets.

Even if you make only minimal adjustments—even if all you do is use tangible book value—you'll already be ahead of most investors. At worst, using only the simple price-to-book value is not a bad anchor to windward, if you also pay attention to the other factors we've covered—like cash flow.

So now you have three important concepts introduced in this chapter:

1. Think about whole companies.
2. Think about cash flows.
3. Think about asset values.

A WORD ABOUT DEBT

There is nothing wrong with debt. It can have many advantages for equity investors.

Scholars of finance love debt, but only because they have no training in credit analysis and fail to see the value of carrying around a little excess capital (a point I'll expand on in the next chapter). Academics look at debt as cheap capital. They like it because interest is tax-deductible. Compared to issuing new shares, debt is almost always cheaper.

In fact, one of my MBA finance professors proclaimed, "If I owned a company I would borrow as much money as lenders would give me." In other words, he would use debt as much as possible and carry around as little equity as possible. Think about owning your house with close to 99 percent debt, as opposed to nearly all equity or very little debt.

Debt may be great in theory and, in certain circumstances, the preferred way to finance things. However, as a public stockholder—in a minority position, in a passive investment, and lacking access to insider information—I've always preferred investing in companies with little or no debt. It's one easy way to create another margin of safety—by covering for business risks. I always sleep better knowing that if something comes out of the dark to surprise me, at least I don't have to worry about the possibility of my company going bankrupt.

Leverage works wonderfully on the way up, but it works with stunning revenge on the way down.

A HIDDEN FOURTH BIG IDEA: HOW TO THINK ABOUT RISK

I wonder if I might call your attention to an observation of the Emperor Marcus Aurelius? He said: "Does aught befall you? It is good. It is part of the destiny of the Universe ordained for you from the beginning. All that befalls you is part of the great web."

"He said that, did he?"

"Yes, sir."

"Well you can tell him from me he's an ass."

     —P. G. Wodehouse, The Mating Season

Risk is a vital part of thinking about investing, even though you can't put a number to it. You can't really start applying many of the ideas in this book without having a good grounding in what makes a risky investment and what makes one investment more or less risky than another.

I think of the concept of risk in terms of enterprise value, cash flows, and asset values. Those three important concepts again. Most investors think about risk in terms of price. They buy a stock, and risk means the probability that the stock price will go down.

By this point, I hope you see that this is not a good conception of risk. You understand now that stock prices are judgments of value that you should not rely on. The public market quotations are going to change in ways that seem irrational. You need something else in which to anchor your concept of risk—and that's your understanding of enterprise value, cash flows, and asset values.

So how should you think about risk?

First, you should understand that risk is more useful with an adjective in front of it—that is, as a specific kind of risk. For example, there are market risks and there are business risks. A market risk is the risk of the stock price moving against you in the short term. We don't worry about this risk, which is the risk of unrealized losses or a reduction in unrealized profits. Market risk is a risk you should ignore.

What we are most interested in is the business risk—a specific risk to the particular business we are looking at. It might be the risk of a big customer leaving or the risk of losing a key contract. It might be the risk of a costly development project not panning out. Business risks can be lots of specific things. What we don't want is a lot of risk that something bad will happen to the business itself.

The great risk we try very hard to avoid is the risk of a *permanent capital impairment*. This is a fancy phrase that captures the idea of a business losing a material amount of money, suffering a severe drop in asset prices, or losing its credit standing. Basically, it is a real material loss that affects what the business can achieve in the long run. A permanent capital impairment shrinks the possibilities of what a business can achieve.

· For example, suffering heavy losses that put the company in bankruptcy is an example of a severe permanent capital impairment. Much will be lost to creditors—if not everything—and the stockholders' interest in the company will be permanently impaired or lessened.

A less severe impairment may be technological obsolescence that has caused a significant piece of the company's business to be worth much less than what was thought. Technology companies usually carry a good amount of this kind of risk that can have you waking up one day to find a competitor has passed you by or an industry has died. If you made typewriters, your business suffered a permanent impairment with the widespread adoption of the computer.

In mining, a permanent capital impairment may be the exhaustion of an important mine; a business in another industry may suffer the loss of a key asset when it is confiscated by a foreign government.

Corporate corruption can lead to permanent impairments. Fraudulent accounting, which leads to a huge write-down of assets, is a permanent capital impairment.

We aim to avoid these risks as best we can. One easy way, as I've already pointed out, is to stick with companies with strong balance sheets and little debt. Without getting too much into accounting details, a strong balance sheet is one in which there is little debt, good liquidity (that is, some idle cash), and not a lot of funny assets—like goodwill (which we strip out in our analysis anyway).

As an aside, you should realize that your goal as an investor should not be to eliminate risk entirely. Every investment brings an element of risk. There is always something that can go wrong.

Even for insiders. There is a common misperception that insiders somehow have a free ride. The thinking is that their information is so good that they can't go wrong. Hence, a number of services have grown up around the idea of following insiders. This can be a very good way to look for potential investments. However, you should realize that insiders face risk when they invest in stocks.

As an outsider, your risk is probably greater, but not always. I have seen insiders who believe so much in their own story that they are the last people to find out when it is no longer valid. They are like the proverbial captains who go down with their ship.

MANAGEMENT CAN BE THE LAST TO KNOW

When I was a commercial lender, I sometimes had to deliver bad news—usually when a company's financial position had deteriorated and I had to get the bank's money back. Basically, I had to tell management we were pulling out.

It was hard because I had spent a lot of time trying to get these people to bank with us—wining and dining them—and I had spend a lot of time building that relationship. Then, always rather suddenly, things started to go sour. As the objective banker, I had to get out.

I can't tell you how many times management took this message as a shock. Even when the deterioration was clear to us at the bank—and

(continues)

MANAGEMENT CAN BE THE LAST TO KNOW *(continued)*

serious enough to threaten the business—management often saw it as only temporary. More often than not, we were right and management was wrong. In a year or two we would find out that the company had been forced to fold or sell out.

In the public stock markets, the same thing happens all the time. Insiders, perhaps so caught up in their own business that they miss the proverbial forest for the trees, simply don't understand the full magnitude of the adversity they face. Many executives are confident, self-made people who have made their living, and their fortune, by overcoming doubters. They are hardly impartial.

Recent events at Lear, an auto parts maker, illustrate the point. Jesse Eisinger wrote an excellent column ("Lear Case Shows Sometimes Investors Can Detect Crises before Management") exploring the case.

Investors had advised Lear's management to pursue certain objectives—like refinancing the company's debts—when times were relatively stable. Most investors saw lots of storm clouds overhead. Disregarding the advice and counsel of their largest shareholder, management continued to pursue their own plans.

Later, as business in the auto parts sector got even worse, management suffered public criticism, as well as a big blow to its credibility, as doubts arose about whether Lear would be able to refinance its heavy debt load. The stock cratered. As Eisinger said, "The company always seems like the last to know."[10]

Message: Don't follow insiders blindly. Managers have blind spots just as investors do.

Insiders Can Get It Wrong

Having said that, insider buying is one of those proven ways of finding good investment ideas. When you see the president, the chief executive officer, and the chief financial officer coming out of pocket and piling into their stock—well, that is worth checking out for yourself.

Insider selling doesn't work so well. Insiders sell for all sorts of personal reasons. Maybe they are simply trying to diversify, or maybe there's a new house or boat they want. Whatever the reason, it's not always a bad sign when insiders sell. Now, if you see several insiders selling heavily as the stock continues to move lower . . . well, that is worth noting and is usually a bad sign.

George Muzea wrote a short book called *The Vital Few versus the Trivial Many.* You can read it in an hour or two. It outlines a good system for using insider buying and selling information. The key, according to Muzea, is divergence from normal insider behavior. "Since it is normal for insiders to buy as their stock goes down and sell as it goes up, we want to look for divergences from this normal behavior," Muzea writes.

> Your eyes should become wide open when you see an insider, especially the Chief Financial Officer who normally sells stock only when the price rises, suddenly break this pattern by selling into weakness.[11]

This could mean there is bad news on the way. Conversely, Muzea says, you should be excited when you see insiders buying at prices higher than their prior purchases. This is usually a bullish sign of the strength of the company's prospects.

An additional consideration is to remember that insiders are not necessarily good investors. They often get it wrong, especially when selling. Even they can't predict the future. In fact, the greatest investor of our age, Warren Buffett, was spectacularly wrong on his own stock in 1996.

In May 1996, Berkshire Hathaway created its B shares, which trade at one-thirtieth the value of the A shares (which never split and are worth $88,000 or so today). Buffett did this to deter promoters from creating low-priced trusts designed to mimic Berkshire's performance. In any event, Buffett issued his most bearish opinions on his stock in the prospectus, saying that Berkshire's shares were not worth buying, "not at this price."

Shortly thereafter, the stock began a strong ascent and doubled in two years.

Again, insiders don't always know when their stock is a good buy. Investors tend to get excited about buybacks, but buybacks can backfire. A classic example of a company that blundered badly in buying back lots of stock without paying attention to the price it paid is Coca-Cola. From 1998 through 2004, the company spent $6 billion of shareholder money to buy back 6 billion shares at an average price of $50.40. There were times during this stretch when the stock was trading for 50 times earnings! Certainly, this was not an intelligent use of shareholder money. And the move has yet to pay off for shareholders: the shares are $43 as I write.

(continues)

MANAGEMENT CAN BE THE LAST TO KNOW *(continued)*

Interpreting what insiders do on the sell side is tricky. And when you see "nonmarket dispositions," that means they have exercised their options—something they routinely do, since these options expire periodically.

Bottom line: Don't get worried just because you see insiders sell some shares from time to time. Often they have little better idea of where the stock is going than you do.

The main way I limit risk, both in what I recommend in *Capital & Crisis* and in my own investing, is to *focus on the downside in my analysis.* What we could make means nothing without having a sense of what we could lose and of the probability of experiencing such a loss. I'm reminded a bit of a Charles Bukowski poem about one of his many visits to the local racetrack. He's sitting there, drinking his beer and watching the horses but not betting. Finally, someone comes up to him and says: "You come here to win, don't you?"

Bukowski's reply was: "I come here not to lose."[12]

In the same way, my focus in the stock market is on not losing. And the best way to do that is to pay a great deal of attention to the price I pay for an investment. In fact, I believe this kind of discipline is the most important part of any investment program.

Here is an example of an investor who did a great job in covering his downside.

INVESTING WHERE OTHERS FEAR TO TREAD: JAMES TISCH

People forget: energy was not always a good business. It goes up and down like a fiddler's elbow, and one day it will be bad again. In the 1980s, things in the oil tanker business weren't just bad—they were nightmarish, especially if you were a ship owner. Indeed, running a tanker business then must have seemed like a pretty good way to blow a wad of money.

It cost around $50 million to build a new ship. Yet you could buy a perfectly good used one for a 90 percent discount—or $5 million. Why? Because only 30 percent of the industry's ships were in use. The rest of them sat around empty, gathering dust and soaking up rays.

Empty ships, you may have gathered, don't bring in any money. And with all those empty ships, even the ships in use were getting terrible rates for their services. The tanker business was not meaningfully profitable.

As a result, ships were trading for scrap value. You could literally buy scrap metal for the same price per tonnage as a fully assembled and working tanker. This wasn't surprising, really. After all, who would want to own oil tankers in those circumstances?

As it turns out, James Tisch did. Tisch is the president and CEO of Loews Corporation. His father, Larry Tisch, is one of the great investors of our time. There is a chapter devoted to him in John Train's book *The Money Masters*. The junior Tisch is proving to be another savvy money mind.

I heard James Tisch relate his story on tankers at the ninth annual Columbia Investment Management Conference held at Columbia University.

Tisch thought that there was little downside risk in tankers then. Any improvement in business could dramatically change the value of tankers, and indeed, the business did improve. Tisch himself made several multiples of his original investment. As I write, tanker companies are gushing money because rates are good, ships are full, and ship owners are awash in cash. The investment paid off big for Tisch.

It's also interesting to note that Tisch's thesis did not depend on some big-picture prediction on oil. In fact, he cautioned conference attendees that he has been wrong many times predicting where oil was going to go. Prediction is not what he does, nor what any successful investor seems to do. If you think about it, it's funny that a craft like investing, which seems all about the future, should have so few successful practitioners who think powers of prediction are important.

Tisch has four basic rules for investing. First, *keep it simple*. The tanker story illustrates the idea that you don't need a complex investment thesis to underpin a great investment. With the tankers,

Tisch was buying well below cost. It's hard to go wrong in such circumstances. Simple ideas are often your best ideas.

Second, *the consensus is often wrong.* Not always, Tisch pointed out, but often. Therefore, you cannot be afraid to back an idea that runs counter to what most experts think.

The third precept Tisch preached was *patience.* He said it is "one of the most important virtues" because great investments "take time to develop and mature."[13]

But above all, Tisch felt that it is most important to *focus on your downside.* If that's covered, then you know you can wait. Opportunities like finding cheap tankers to buy come along only once in a while. But the basic lessons behind Tisch's story and his precepts are good for investors to digest and remember.

Part of the reason to limit your downside is based in a practical and mathematical reality. The different amounts that result after compounding over 5 or 10 years are huge, even if the different rates of compounding are relatively small—say, between 10 and 12 percent, or between 6 and 8 percent. At higher rates, every time you suffer a big loss you *dramatically lower* your potential future returns.

To reduce risk—to reduce the risk of a loss or a permanent capital impairment—you have to focus on the price paid. We'll get into the nuts and bolts of valuation in the next chapter, but first I want to dispel a misconception about the relationship between risk and return.

A COMMON MISPERCEPTION ABOUT RISK AND REWARD

> *To the extent most investors think about risk at all, they seem confused about it. Some insist that risk and return are always positively correlated; the greater the risk, the greater the return. This is, in fact, a basic tenet of the capital asset pricing model taught in nearly all business schools, yet it is not always true.*
>
> —*Seth Klarman*[14]

In business school, everyone is taught that risk and reward go together. When you take bigger risks, you make more money. And when you take smaller dosages of risk, you get less return. This is often taught as a law.

Reality, though, doesn't work that way. In fact, you will find value-rich opportunities in profitable companies that are in rock-solid financial condition. These are low-risk situations, and yet they will make you a lot of money. Conversely, you could invest in a blue-chip stock that everyone praises—Fortune, Money, Morningstar, whoever—and it might still be, by my lights, a risky holding. It's risky either because of a high valuation (the usual case) or because of a weak financial condition that the mainstream doesn't get (like Fannie Mae or, worse, something like Enron when it was hot). And you will find that these risky plays lose you a lot of money.

I'm not stating any general laws. I'm just advising that you toss out the idea that risk and return must go together.

AGRIUM: HOW A SERIES OF FORTUNATE EVENTS BUILT A $2 BILLION BUSINESS

In the end, they were $300,000 apart, which in 1898 was real money.

On one side of the negotiating table was Frederick Augustus Heinze, the illustrious American copper magnate. The "Boy Wonder" was only 29, but already a celebrity among the business barons of the day. The Brooklyn-born entrepreneur was, by all accounts, brilliant, uncompromising, dashing—and very rich.

On the other side of the table was Walter Hull Aldridge, a bright metallurgist, representing the Canadian Pacific Railroad. Aldridge, only a couple of years older, had a few things in common with Heinze. He, too, was Brooklyn-born, and Aldridge also attended the prestigious Columbia University School of Mines. The similarities, though, would seem to end there, for while Aldridge would quietly go on to have a successful career, he never achieved the fantastic fame and wealth of Heinze. Aldridge, though, had an interesting bloodline: he was a descendant of Commodore Isaac Hull, whose USS *Constitution* so bedeviled British ships in the War of 1812.

At issue between them was a copper smelter Heinze owned in Trail, British Columbia, along with a short-line railroad called the Columbia & Western (C&W).

The Canadian Pacific Railroad was feeling its oats about this time, having generated a substantial profit the year before, its trains laden

(continues)

**AGRIUM: HOW A SERIES OF FORTUNATE EVENTS
BUILT A $2 BILLION BUSINESS** *(continued)*

with incoming settlers and filled with freight. Flush with cash to invest, the railroad had visions of expanding across western Canada, hauling coal, coke, wheat, machinery, lumber, and metals across the resource-rich region.

The Canadian Pacific was interested in Heinze's rail because it fit nicely in their plans. Late in 1897, they made an offer for it. Heinze, though, wouldn't sell just the railroad. He would sell the whole shebang—smelter and rail—or he wouldn't sell at all. His asking price was $1.2 million. Heinze was running a bluff, because his Canadian operations were not doing so well and his American interests demanded his attention. The Trail operation's outlook was not so bright, either, with the threat of competing smelters being built in the area.

Canadian Pacific wanted the C&W badly enough, however, and finally agreed to include the smelter in their offer, and now they were struggling to meet Heinze's price.

The two negotiators worked late into the cold night of February 11, 1898, and reached an impasse. Heinze offered to play poker for the difference, which was about $300,000. Aldridge—wisely, I think—declined. Heinze had a reputation as a good poker player.

Eventually, Canadian Pacific swallowed hard and met Heinze's price. Just like that, the Canadian Pacific Railroad was in the smelter business. Aldridge stayed on as managing director of the company that the railroad created to house the smelter. Under Aldridge's direction, the smelter not only supplied copper, but by 1902 it was also putting out pure lead and fine gold and silver.

The acquisition of the smelter was fortunate event number one. With the financial muscle of the railroad behind it, the smelter's capabilities were upgraded and expanded. It proved to be one of the best investments of the old Canadian Pacific. By 1925 the plant at Trail covered some 250 acres, employed over 2,000 men, and earned a record $37 million—ironic, considering it was originally only a throw-in, a sort of bitter concession to the forceful Heinze.

There was only one problem: it was making people sick. The fruit tress didn't bear fruit, and the vegetables tasted funny. The noxious fumes that had soaked the surrounding area for years had finally become intolerable to surrounding residents. After legal action, the company began to make modifications to reduce the poisonous emissions from its smelter.

Here again, serendipity would have a role to play. The filters the company applied captured dusts that could be used to make fertilizers. So the company built a fertilizer plant, and by 1931 the company could offer hydrogen, nitrogen, ammonia, and other like products. This was fortunate event number two. It was this initial foray into fertilizers that eventually became Agrium (NYSE: AGU).

Agrium was a company I recommended in January 2005. It was one of the largest producers of commercial fertilizers, euphemistically known as nutrients. The primary nutrients are nitrogen, phosphate, and soluble potash. Nitrogen is part of every plant's DNA and is most commonly used to increase crop yields. Phosphate is also part of plant DNA and helps the plant use water effectively, promotes root development, improves grain quality, and accelerates ripening. Potash, or potassium, is critically important to the process of photosynthesis—or the processing of sugars in the plant. It also helps to make plants hardy, improving their ability to weather disease and withstand the stress of drought. Other nutrients used in smaller amounts, called micronutrients, include iron, zinc, copper, and boron. All of these nutrients replenish the soil to maintain or enhance its fertility.

The thesis behind the recommendation was fairly simple. More people, with more money in their pocket (particularly in emerging markets like China and India and even Brazil), meant more money spent on meat. More meat means more livestock, which requires more feed. More feed means more corn and more fertilizers. Fortunately, the rationale for owning Agrium did not depend solely on a bullish analysis of the fertilizer market, as you will soon see.

As I went to press with my recommendation, Agrium likely ended 2004 with $400 million in cash, producing $500 million in EBITDA, and $300 million in operating cash flow during the year. Put another way, nearly one-fifth of the company's market cap was in cash, and it traded for only five times its estimated 2004 EBITDA.

The demands on that cash flow are relatively light. Capital expenditures required to maintain the business are around $90 million annually. Therefore, the company probably threw off over $200 million in free cash flow in 2004. These numbers are strong and reflect the tight

(continues)

**AGRIUM: HOW A SERIES OF FORTUNATE EVENTS
BUILT A $2 BILLION BUSINESS *(continued)***

global supply-and-demand situation for nutrients, particularly nitrogen
and potash.[15]

This piece was originally published in February 2005. By March 2007,
the stock price had soared, handing in a gain of over 160 percent for
Capital & Crisis readers. Again, the point of the example is to show how
cash flow and a strong financial condition made Agrium a safe bet—even
though the business is in a cyclical industry and even though it had lost
money the year before (on an earnings basis).

WORKING THE PIECES TOGETHER

The tools in this chapter—concepts like enterprise value, cash flows,
asset values, and financial strength, and thinking differently about risk—
are all critical tools for me as an investor and for many of the greats.
These tools expose weaknesses in many popular ratios and ideas.

With the basic ideas in this chapter, you will be less interested in
price-earnings ratios, moving averages, and other simple numbers. I
hope you will find a new calm and confidence in your investing. You
won't worry about daily changes in stock prices. This investing stuff is
actually a lot of fun. You don't have to rush it. It's like a great big puzzle you can assemble at your leisure. You'll learn lots about the companies you own, and this knowledge will just build up over time.
Before you know it, you'll surprise yourself with what you know.

CHAPTER 3

CREATING WEALTH— OR WHAT MAKES STOCKS RISE

Since the first modern exchange opened for business in Amsterdam in the seventeenth century, investors have been asking themselves the same big question: "What will go up?"

Back then, Josef Penso de la Vega, a businessman and writer, roamed the bourse, perhaps speculating on the shares of the Dutch East India Company and wondering about the price of herrings and whale oil. De la Vega did us a great favor by writing a book called *Confusión de Confusiónes*, which gives us important insights into the markets of the time.

He was also somewhat poetic in his descriptions. "The bulls are like the giraffe which is scared of nothing," he wrote, "or like the magician . . . who in his mirror made the ladies appear much more beautiful than they were in reality. They love everything, they praise everything." The bears, on the other hand, "were completely ruled by fear, trepidation and nervousness. Rabbits become elephants, brawls in a tavern become rebellions, faint shadows to them appear as signs of chaos."[1]

De la Vega advised being neither a bull nor a bear, but an opportunist. "Trim one's sails according to the wind," he said. De la Vega wrote about how stock prices could take big swings based on news and gossip. How a fall in stock prices caused more sellers to surface from frightened investors just as the "leaves tremble in the softest breeze.""Clever people," he wrote, "make skillful uses of these advantages."[2]

Markets are no different today. There are still panicky sellers, and there are still opportunists who take advantage of market prices—as opposed to letting those market prices dictate their actions.

And the answer to the basic question of what will go up—and stay up over time—is this: *whatever creates wealth over the long term*. The focus of investing is long-term wealth creation.

Companies create wealth in more ways than simply generating ever-higher earnings per share. And investors stand to make money in more ways than simply owning shares of companies that report ever-higher earnings per share. In fact, if you focus only on earnings per share, you miss out on a lot of stuff. Most investors miss out.

Consider the old railroads. They were the stocks to own for a long stretch of time. They boomed as the nation filled out its middle and the economies of the states became more integrated. For many years the rail companies produced great earnings.

But then there was a period of decline. Earnings struggled, then declined, and rail companies began to disappear.

This kind of thing frightens investors looking at earnings per share. And indeed, many were doing just that. But what they overlooked was the vast land holdings of the rail companies. These land holdings later became timber operations, warehouse properties, oil and gas reserves, home building tracts, and much more.

Arguably, the wealth spawned by the old railroads' land holdings exceeded their contributions as railroads.

Catellus Development Corporation was a company I recommended to my readers in 2004. It had a railroad heritage, stretching back to the old Santa Fe railroad. As a spin-off from the railroad, Catellus owned land that happened to be around key distribution centers in several major cities, and Catellus had built warehouses on this land. The old railroad's locations—again, key distribution points in important cities—proved a wealthy treasure trove for Catellus to mine for years. ProLogis eventually bought it out in 2005—and we pocketed a nice 21 percent gain in only eight months.

This is one example. Real estate is an example people understand more intuitively. So we'll start with that.

There are companies that own significant land holdings or significant real estate. Sometimes it is incidental to the business—for example, a retailer that happens to own the land its stores operate on. Sometimes it is very much a part of the business—for example, a hotel company.

In either case, any increase in the value of the real estate does not show up in earnings per share. Over time, of course, the value of the real estate could be huge—indeed, it could dwarf the value of the underlying businesses, as happened with the railroads. Such opportunities are usually rare, as you would expect. Nonetheless, opportunities occasionally surface.

Real estate is just one example, as I've said, of a company creating wealth outside of the usual earnings per share that investors so lovingly follow. There are many more ways, however, in which companies can create wealth.

In this chapter, we'll explore this idea and how this focus changes the way you invest.

FOUR BIG WAYS INVESTORS WIN

The man who made this all crystal clear to me, and to whom I will forever be indebted, is Martin Whitman of Third Avenue, and the author of a couple of great books on investing—though be forewarned: they are not easy reading.

In his book *Value Investing*, Whitman describes four ways in which companies create value or wealth:

1. Earnings
2. Free cash flow
3. Resource conversion
4. Access to capital markets

Let's look at each one in a bit more detail.

Earnings from Operations

This is the wealth creation method that most investors think of. They think of a company producing growing earnings over many years—the

great companies like McDonald's, Wal-Mart, and Microsoft just cranking out earnings year after year. No doubt, this is a wealth creator.

Earnings are not cash, as I've shown. But the creation of legitimate
earnings, even if no cash is immediately produced, is a way to create
wealth. Because at some point in the future those earnings will convert to cash.

Let's say that the earnings generated are largely reinvested in the
business. The earnings are tied up in receivable and inventories, and
what's left over is plowed back into new stores and expansion efforts.
This in turn creates even more earnings, and the process repeats.
Maybe at the end of ten years, or twenty years, the enterprise starts to
slow down.

Then, because money is not needed to reinvest as heavily as in the
past, the business throws off gobs of cash flow.

This takes us to the second way to create wealth.

Free Cash Flow from Operations

The curious thing about the wealth-creating power of earnings is how
much cash is consumed—think of all that money tied up in working
capital (inventory, receivables) and all the money required for reinvestment in the business. Since earnings consume cash, earnings alone do
not create wealth unless earnings eventually lead to the creation of free
cash flow.

Free cash flow means that an excess of cash is generated over the
amount required for the business. This is money left over after accounts
receivable, inventory, and reinvestment needs are met. The notion of
"free" means that the company could distribute it in the form of dividends, buy back stock, or let the money pile up on the balance sheet
in its bank account.

Whitman contends that very few companies actually produce free
cash flow. Most companies are ongoing concerns engaged in expansion efforts—and thus create earnings.

Free cash flow creates value for good reasons. If you were going to
own a piece of a business, you would probably value highly that business's ability to generate cash. Who wants to own a business that does
not throw off cash—and shows no prospects of ever doing so?

If you follow the approach in this book, you are concerned about
cash flow. You want cash flow—lots of present or future cash flow—for

the price you pay for the business. Ideally, you get lots of cash flow today for money you pay today, and you don't have to rely on the vagaries of the future. But I will not rule out the possibility that you will find really strong businesses worth paying up for. Their positions or businesses are so strong that they are likely to crank out much higher amounts of cash in the future.

In any event, if you stop your analysis here—and think about cash flows instead of just thinking about earnings—you will already be well ahead of most investors. If you want to take your "game" to another level, continue on.

Resource Conversion Activities

This includes a lot of things: converting assets to higher uses, operating under other ownership or control, or both; financing asset acquisitions, refinancing liabilities, or both. Under this umbrella is the whole edifice of mergers, acquisitions, restructurings, and more.

Sounds complex. It doesn't have to be so complex. And you don't have to be able to analyze *all* of this stuff to bring *some* of it into your investment style. Understanding just some of the basics can go a long way in helping you find winners.

Generally speaking, "resource conversion" as a way of creating wealth means that you can create wealth by shuffling around your assets or liabilities in new ways or combinations. Let's consider some examples.

The obvious way, again, is using real estate. A company that runs fast-food chains and also owns the real estate its locations occupy may one day find itself sitting on a gold mine in unrecognized real estate value.

It may be that the company would be better off selling its real estate and using that huge amount of cash for something else. Or it may be better for shareholders to spin off the real estate assets under another corporate umbrella, new stock and all. The announcement of such moves can lead to dramatically higher stock prices, and such structures can create a lot of value over time—more so than if the old structure persisted.

Or a company may be sitting on a lot of excess cash not appropriately recognized by the market, which values the company essentially in line with other less well-endowed competitors. This is another situation I love.

All that excess cash could be used to buy back stock, pay a special dividend, or whatever. Companies like this are often takeover candidates. The pile of cash represents real value. You can invest in these situations with the idea that value could be unlocked sometime in the future because of conversion activities.

To some extent, you make these decisions on a certain kind of faith. You won't know for sure that management will do anything. They may fight hard for the status quo, and no one may even challenge them on it.

However, as competitive as the markets are, many of these kinds of opportunities work out, even keeping in mind the fact that you may wind up with some duds. And certainly, these kinds of conversion activities go through periods of ebb and flow. I believe we are in the midst of a long-term trend during which corporate activism will press many firms to engage in conversion activities.

Resource conversion is about more than just a real estate play. I've used that example because it's the most intuitive. Whitman lists a couple of others in his book.

Take financial or insurance companies with excess capital. These companies could redeploy these assets in other areas and generate better returns. Other companies could acquire them.

New ownership may pay a substantial premium to own an asset. For example, if you have a company whose main focus is real estate and it happens to own a substantial interest in a nickel mine, then you have the potential for conversion profits—selling the mine at a big premium to a nickel producer.

There is really a lot here. Some of it will become more apparent as we go along. I could write a whole book on conversion activities alone.

Suffice to say, the most important point here is simply this: When you are looking at investments, consider the resources the company owns—cash, land, other assets—even if they are tangential to the ongoing operations of the company and even if they are not primarily involved in creating earnings. There is much wealth to be made in other ways.

Sometimes you'll find a company that is suffering from nasty short-term earnings worries but that owns top-quality assets. Such a company can be bought cheap because people worry about short-term earnings, even when the long term looks pretty good. These kinds of situations are great opportunities.

Also, because fewer investors seem to be looking at companies in terms of potential conversion activities, it's an area with comparatively less competition than the field of those guessing what next quarter's earnings will be.

The main impetus driving most conventional investors is the idea that businesses should be valued strictly as going concerns. Or, as Whitman writes:

> Corporations are seen as devoted essentially to the same day-to-day operations they have always operated, managed and controlled as they have always been managed and controlled and financed pretty much as they always have been financed. . . . It is likely that the going concern assumption never accurately described most U.S. corporations with publicly traded securities.[3]

He goes on to say:

> It seems unlikely that few U.S. corporations are going to go as long as 5 years without being involved in resource conversion activities, such as mergers and acquisitions; changes of control; management buyouts; massive share repurchases; major financings, refinancings, or reorganizations; sales of assets in bulk; spinoffs; investment in new ventures in other industries; and corporate liquidations.[4]

That is all well put by Whitman. I'll add that all these conversion activities can have big impacts on how a company is valued in the marketplace. So, given, as Whitman says, that few companies go long without having these kinds of things happen, it would seem to make sense to try to understand these activities—and to take them into consideration at least as much as earnings per share. Focusing only on earnings per share is too narrow a focus and misses a great deal of this activity.

In the approach in this book, we look at the many different ways a company could evolve or change, and that analysis must take into account the quality and quantity of the company's resources that could be used in conversion activities.

Access to Capital Markets on a Super-Attractive Basis

Whitman writes, "It seems probable that more corporate wealth, and certainly wealth for financiers, is created by this route than any other."[5] When a company accesses the capital markets, it is trying to raise money—by either selling shares or borrowing money. If you think about the many billions raised in the initial public offerings and the massive amounts of corporate debt that have been sold over the years, it's not hard to imagine that Whitman is right.

In any event, companies can create wealth by accessing the capital markets at super-attractive rates. If you have the ability to tap into the bond markets and raise debt at, let's say, a 5 percent rate when most people have to pay 7 to 8 percent, you have the ability to create wealth where others cannot. Your lower financing costs translate into better cash flows on your investments. In addition, this ability allows you to swing deals and take advantage of opportunities that are unavailable to others because they don't have the financial strength.

Summary of the Four Ways in Which Companies Create Wealth—And How Stockholders Benefit

These are the four basic ways in which companies create wealth—earnings, free cash flow, resource conversion, and access to capital markets.

As an investor, you benefit when:

- Increased cash flows lead to increased dividends or other cash payments to stockholders
- Increased earnings and cash flow lead to increased prices that other investors are willing to pay for these investments (including higher multiples of cash flow and earnings)
- The gap between business values and stock prices in the public markets narrows

More Points from Whitman on "Going Concern" versus "Resource Conversion"

This seems like a good place to stick in a few words about the general idea of evaluating businesses on a going-concern basis versus looking at resource conversion. The public markets—and most investors—are solely devoted to the going-concern analysis. That is, they concern themselves only with the company continuing pretty much as is.

However, given the wide number of ways in which a company can create wealth through resource conversion activities, and given that few companies will continue along without changing over the years, resource conversion should be a part of an investor's analysis.

In my banking career, we always considered resource conversion, although we didn't call it that. We typically looked at deals in terms of primary and secondary (and sometimes tertiary) sources of repayment.

The primary source of repayment was nearly always cash flow from operations. This was basically a going-concern analysis: we looked at the company and what it was, as well as at the industry, competitors, assessed risks, and so on. The secondary source of repayment was usually some kind of collateral, the value of which often involved an analysis of the company in a liquidation scenario or in some sort of resource conversion activity—perhaps involving the sale of real estate to another entity, which might or might not have been engaged in the same business.

For example, one of our biggest customers was a lumber company. It owned real estate in a prime location in a suburb outside of Washington, DC. In evaluating the property this company owned, we had to consider what it would be worth to other businesses and buyers in the event that the bank had to foreclose and sell the asset. In this case, the asset was probably worth a lot more to another business—like a retailer or grocery store—than it was to another lumber company. The likely buyer would be a business or developer. This represented a hidden source of value in the lumberyard. The lumber company was primed for resource conversion–type activities to unlock value in the future—if needed.

Still, like most things in investing, there are trade-offs.

Looking at a company as both a going concern and a source of resource conversion can lead to very different analyses. As Whitman writes: "Frequently, what is right for resource conversion is wrong for a going concern, and vice versa."[6]

Whitman gives the example of Japanese insurers in 1997. Their main asset was a portfolio of loans and stocks. On a resource conversion basis, they looked attractive, since they could be bought for less than the net asset value of these securities.

However, on a going-concern basis, they didn't look so good. They traded for price-earnings ratios of 20 or higher, and their outlooks were clouded and worrisome.

Depending on what sort of analysis you have emphasized, you could come to vastly different conclusions. Whitman's more comprehensive view was the right one, and these investments subsequently made a lot of money for his shareholders as their outlooks improved over time.

As Whitman likes to say, "Any passive investment has something wrong with it, and good analysts spend a lot of time trying to figure out what is wrong and worrying about it."[7]

But just because an investment has something wrong with it doesn't mean it can't be a great investment.

Finally, let's consider the tax implications of creating wealth. Whitman writes:

> The most inefficient tax way to create wealth is to have reportable operating earnings, a *going concern emphasis*; the most efficient way to create wealth is to have unrealized (and therefore mostly unreported) appreciation of asset values, a *resource conversion emphasis* [italics added].[8]

Got that? It's more tax-efficient to create wealth by holding on to an asset that appreciates—tax-free—than to create regularly reported and taxable earnings. Of course, most companies have no choice. But now you, with your new keen eye for resource conversion opportunities, will ferret out opportunities well ahead of the crowd.

In my newsletter, I have emphasized resource conversion investments—but not always. At times there are very good and interesting plays that lack a resource conversion angle.

It usually doesn't pay to be too doctrinaire about investing concepts. It's always good to look at each investment on its own merits. However, the central thrust of this book is to give you some ways to find great investments and understand wealth creation—concepts not well covered in the mainstream literature.

THE THEORY OF SLACK

All of this folds into a working theory I have been developing. I call it "the theory of slack." The basic idea is that owning companies that have *lots of capacity*—whether in excess cash or excess assets—and *low amounts of liabilities*—whether in debts or pending litigation or growing pension obligations—is a great way to make big profits in stocks. This combination of lots of capacity and low amounts of liabilities represents the amount of *slack* a company has.

The theory of slack simply posits that slack in and of itself is a valuable commodity. The reason it's valuable is because greater amounts of slack make it easier for you to pursue those wealth-generating activities I've been outlining. Resource conversion—for instance, a big stock buyback—is easier and more likely when you have lots of cash and assets to use for that purpose. Creating additional earnings and cash flow is easier if you've already got a lot of capacity to do that when the opportunity arrives. If your market gets hot, your business has the ability to capitalize on it, whereas a company with resource constraints—not enough cash, too much debt to borrow more, too little capacity without additional time and money to add more capacity—can't capitalize on the opportunity.

Ironically, many companies with a lot of slack trade cheaply. The market tends to undervalue slack. The market likes companies that are run tight and where every asset is producing coin and debt is used to create leverage and power things like return on equity—another of the Street's favorite tools. The market is often impatient and does not look favorably on a company that is not firing on all cylinders.

So, not only does slack provide ways to increase wealth, but the slack itself tends to be cheap in the market. One day I plan to do more empirical research on this idea and flesh it out, but for now I can say that logically and by the light of my own experience, the theory of slack has found many winners for me.

THE ART OF BUSINESS VALUATION

Out of necessity, I'm not going to say a lot here about business valuation. I harbor no illusions about being able to teach you the art of business valuation in a short book like this. Whole books have been written about nothing but business valuation.

One is Aswath Damodaran's *Investment Valuation*. Damodaran discusses a variety of investment tools and the strengths and weaknesses of different models. It's hard work learning valuation, but there are only a few basic models. Everything else is added bells and whistles.

None of these models are perfect, and different people work better with different tools, just like some artists are great with a paintbrush and others are better with a pencil. There is no perfect way to do any of this.

In a later chapter where I talk about where to look for investments, I'll give you some shortcuts. For the moment, I want to make some general comments about valuation.

The first is that valuation is an art, not a science. There is no right answer, and there is no exact number. Right off the bat, purge your mind of the desire to find an exact value and a right answer. Keep an open mind and be prepared to deal with a lot vagaries and a lot of gray area.

All the earnings, cash flows, and asset numbers you work with are themselves approximations put together by accountants adhering to a set of rules, assumptions, and guidelines. With different accounting treatments and different applications of guidelines, the same company could report very different results. So the basic tools themselves are not precise instruments. But that doesn't make them useless. In fact, you can tell a person's age and weight and height with a fairly reasonable standard of accuracy just by looking at them, without any scales or measurements or personal information.

Valuing companies is not too different from that. Over time you'll get better and better at it.

Even when you do get good at valuing businesses, the fact is that the number itself changes over time. New information and ever-changing markets impact business valuations. This means you may have to revisit your assumptions every so often, depending on how important the new information is. And let's face it: Forecasts are wrong. Things happen that we never expected. No one could have factored in the impact of September 11 on American business, to take an extreme example. There are many unknowns and many unknowables.

The precision of computers these days has added a layer of superficial precision to valuation. Today anybody with a spreadsheet can run a discounted cash flow valuation that is sophisticated, detailed . . . and wrong.

All these numbers and all this rigor give the illusion of certainty. I would urge investors to think in terms of ranges or broad generalities and to demand a good cushion between your estimate and the market price. A business may be worth between $40 and $48 per share. If it's trading at $39, that's nothing to get too excited about. It may still be a great investment, but just recognize that your own estimate is pretty close to the market. If you're going to emphasize safety, you'll want a good 25 percent cushion or more. The greater the cushion, the more safety you have—but also the fewer investment choices.

I like to work with around 40 percent. My own valuations tend to be conservative, and the companies I look at usually have a lot of ways to win for me. I'll get tighter if the business is truly a strong, top-notch business that I want to own for a very long time. Some businesses rarely—if ever—reach wide discounts from underlying value. For those truly great businesses, you may decide the price is good enough and hold on.

Generally speaking, the less you can pay for one dollar of cash flow or one dollar of asset value the better. That's a very broad statement, because cash flows and asset values are difficult to determine. For example, to accurately gauge the value of a business on a cash flow basis, you would have to forecast cash flows for many years out into the future—a kind of predicting that no one does well.

So, as best as possible, you're looking to pick up bargains based on conditions today, without relying too heavily on future growth to make your valuation work.

Even so, not all growth is created equally. Growth has many sources. "For any particular business," Klarman writes

> earnings growth can stem from increased unit sales related to predictable increases in the general population, to increased usage of a product by consumers, to increased market share, to greater penetration of a product into the population or to price increases.[9]

It's helpful to think about what type of growth you're betting on, because different types of growth are more predictable than others. Growth based on population growth is a better bet, for example, than growth based on taking business from competitors.

In the next chapter, I'm going to show you some places to look for good investment ideas.

CHAPTER 4

HUNTING GROUNDS

A blind pig can sometimes find truffles, but it helps to know that they are found in oak forests.

—David Ogilvy

Every generation has its "new age" or "new era." These catchphrases liberally salt financial history. Even in the 1930s, during the Great Depression, one could make a case that a "new era of innovation" was afoot. Social historian Frederick Lewis Allen, in his retrospective book on the 1930s, *Since Yesterday* (originally published in 1939), gives us ample evidence of exactly that.

"There were visible promises," Allen writes, "if one looked about one, of what might prove to be a new industrial age."[1] He writes about sleek new trains made of duralumin and stainless steel. By 1936 there were 358 cars in operation or under construction, and they attracted crowds that marveled at this "symbol of the new America" wherever they went. Moreover, these cars were air-conditioned—as were an increasing number of restaurants, shops, and movie theaters.

The automobile manufacturers turned out cars with sweeping curves and stunning bulges. They were streamlined, more efficient, more comfortable, and faster than any cars before them. They drove on new highways with cloverleaf intersections and overpasses, zipping about to different towns faster than had ever before been possible.

Ocean liners set new speed records and also topped previous marks for size. And what about airplanes? "The great silvery Douglas DC-3 of

June 1936," Allen tells us, "had a cruising speed of 200 mph [compared with] the 100 mph transport planes of 1932."[2]

People would take tours of Rockefeller Center in New York, one of the impressive skyscrapers to rise in the United States during the 1930s. They would wonder at the gleaming new materials and dreamily imagine the skyline of a new metropolis.

The innovators then were not software developers or computer manufacturers. They were chemists and metallurgists producing new and lighter materials, including steels; mixing nickel, chromium, tungsten, and other metals; and creating plastics and new fibers.

People fell in love with technology and the world of tomorrow, as they had in years past and as they still do today. The hunt for the next big thing and the never-quenchable thirst to get rich quick propelled investors to spin out great theories of what the future would look like. But unlike armchair philosophers and hobby futurologists, they backed these visions with their money.

"Was there, perhaps, some new machine, some new gadget, the furious demand for which would set in motion the boom," Allen wondered, "something like the automobile or the radio?"[3] In the 1930s, investors thought they had found it in, of all things, prefabricated housing.

According to Allen, a bacteriologist named Arthur Sherman built a house on wheels that he could pull behind his car when his family went on vacations. It attracted a lot of attention, and he built more and displayed them at the Detroit Auto Show in 1930. Before long, he was making "trailers" on a larger scale, and hundreds of other manufacturers jumped in. People started living in them year-round.

By 1936 the number of trailers surged to 160,000 by some estimates. Perhaps the peak happened on New Year's Day. Florida observers counted trailers entering the state at the rate of 25 per hour. Economist Roger Babson declared that half of the population would be living in trailers within the next 20 years.

What a vision, Allen notes, "provided one did not focus one's attention on real estate values, taxes, steady jobs, schooling for the children, sanitation problems and other such prosy details."[4]

By 1937 the trailer boom collapsed under the weight of a saturated market and misplaced optimism. It also got caught in a larger economic crisis. A big break in the stock market cut the Dow Jones industrial average in half, from a high of 195 in March 1937 to a sickening low of 97.46 by March 1938—so much for the next new thing.

"The history of the stock market is the history of forgetting," wrote that market sage F. J. Chu in his book *The Mind of the Market*.[5] Anecdotal evidence is seen in how soon the 1937–1938 collapse followed on the heels of its more famous cousin, the 1929–1932 debacle. How quickly investors forget; how wicked is the bear market at work.

Financial survivors of the 1937–1938 meltdown were like the survivors of other panics—they had cash and little debt; they were patient; and they stuck with the tried-and-true, having shunned the latest investment fads.

Many of the investments in the new technology of the 1930s failed to deliver profits to investors, at least immediately, just as the billions poured into technology stocks in the late 1990s never saw much of a return, if any.

The lesson in all of this is simply that what is hot and popular—and often banking heavily on the foggy unknowable world of tomorrow—is not a good place to go looking for your next investments.

WHERE TO LOOK

Now that you have some conceptual idea of the kinds of investments to look for, you're ready to go hunting. This chapter highlights some fertile areas for finding good investments. The basic idea behind all of these strategies is to look for names. To be a good investor and get good returns, you have to go through a lot of names.

It's like being on one of those old trains where some industrious fellow has to keep shoveling in the coal to keep it going. It's the same with investors: You need a constant steady stream of names and ideas to investigate further. Be prepared to turn over a lot of rocks and say no to a lot of ideas before you settle on one. Then the process starts all over again.

But this is the fun part. This is the part all great investors love—the intellectual challenge and the thrill of the hunt. It's a great adventure, and if you are bored with it or don't have time for it, then find somebody who does and lean on them (like me!).

Now, without further ado, let me show you some of my favorite hunting grounds.

HUNTING GROUND #1: TAKING A PEEK AT WHAT THE GREATS ARE DOING

What the greats are doing is easily my all-time favorite hunting ground, and the source of countless good ideas over the years. Following this method is not difficult, either. You simply compile a list of portfolio managers whom you greatly respect and who have done very well. Then you go to their websites, read their annual and quarterly letters, and find out what they are holding and what they are buying.

You can also go to the SEC's web page (www.sec.gov) and search for the company by name. For example, one of my favorite investors is Seth Klarman. The name of his firm is Baupost Group LLC. When you type in "Baupost," you see a number of Baupost firms listed. Click on "Baupost Group LLC" and look at the statement filed there called "Quarterly Report Filed by Institutional Managers: Holdings."

When you click on that and scroll down, you see his whole portfolio. Pretty neat, huh? It's like peeking over the shoulder of one of the all-time greats as he works. Then you can take that list and voila! You have a list of stocks to research and follow.

Now, people will criticize this approach and say, "Well, you don't know when they bought it or what they paid . . . and they could sell it without you knowing, and then you're hosed."

Well, these people are half right. You could, with a little digging, find out what Baupost paid (roughly) and when it bought the stock. And you can also see whether Baupost is adding to its position or subtracting. But that shouldn't matter so much.

You have to decide whether it is worth buying now. Scary though it may seem, you have to pull the trigger on any buy based on your own reasons and conviction. Otherwise, the next time the stock takes a dip, you'll get scared out of it. Worse, you won't know when to sell.

The concept here is to find a good "hunting ground"—not as a way to just automatically duplicate the portfolios of your favorite money managers but as a really good place to look for ideas.

The next section is a piece I wrote in early 2006 about a group of investors who have proved their mettle: the fifteen best funds of the last 15 years. Because their records teach us a lesson about investment performance, they are fifteen good names to get started with.

The Miller Record

Miller, the steward of the Legg Mason Value Trust, beat the S&P 500 for 15 years running. Journalists spilled a lot of ink celebrating this streak. But really, how important is such a record? Is the pursuit of regular market-beating gains a worthy goal?

I don't mean to take anything away from Miller, but I remember when I spent some time with another investment great, Ralph Wanger—who managed the Acorn Fund for years—and he told me, with a wink, that Miller's record was nice and all, but look who's beaten him over that span (see Table 4.1).

TABLE 4.1   Best Funds of the Last 15 Years

Rank	Fund	Annual Total Return	Manager Name
1	FPA Capital	20.0%	Robert L. Rodriguez
2	Fidelity Lw-Prcd Stk	18.8	Joel Tillinghast
3	Calamos: Growth A	18.3	N. Calamos
4	Heartland: Value	18.1	Nasgovitz
5	Columbia Acorn: Z	18.0	McQuaid/Mohn
6	ICM Small Co: Inst	17.6	Robert McDorman
7	Hartfd: Cap App HLS: IA	17.5	Saul Pannell
8	DFA US Micro Cap	17.1	Team-managed
9	Merrill Value Oppty: I	17.1	R. Elise Baum
10	Muhlenkamp	17.1	Ron H. Muhlenkamp
11	Federated Kaufmann: K	16.9	Auriana/Utsch
12	H&W: Small Cap Value: I	16.9	Jim Miles
13	Janus Sm Cap Val: Inst	16.9	Perkins/Perkins
14	Neuberger Genesis: Inv	16.9	D'Alelio/Vale
15	Laudus Ro US SC: Inst	16.8	William Ricks
16	Wasatch: Core Growth	16.7	J. B. Taylor
17	Mairs & Power Growth	16.6	William B. Frels
18	Third Avenue: Value	16.5	Martin J. Whitman
19	Skyline: Special Eq	16.5	William Fiedler
20	Legg Mason Val Tr: Prm	16.4	Bill Miller

Total return is for December 31, 1990, through December 31, 2005.

Indeed, there are 19 funds—but only 11 with the same manager for the whole run—that beat Miller's fund over the last 15 years, even though they did not beat the market every year. That fact may surprise you. Yet, look back over the track records of great investors and you find their meaty returns were not consistent. Creating investing returns is not like mixing flour, yeast, and eggs to make bread. It's like using a recipe and only sometimes getting what you expect. Sometimes you get something much more, sometimes much less.

I recently read Barton Biggs's book *Hedgehogging*. Biggs was with Morgan Stanley for thirty years, during which time he created their research department and became a national figure as an investment strategist. *Hedgehogging* is an entertaining and impressionistic memoir that covers a lot of ground. But one piece in the book really brings home this idea that you don't have to beat the market every year. *Indeed, most of the greats rarely do.*

Biggs writes about Warren Buffett's famous essay "The Superinvestors of Graham-and-Doddsville." In this essay, Buffett refutes the idea—popular among academics—that the stock market is efficiently priced and beating it is largely a matter of luck. He then goes through the track records of 10 investment management firms that crushed the market over time. Each of these firms is committed to the approach begun by Benjamin Graham and David Dodd, but since elaborated upon and improved by many others.

Biggs, though, focuses on another facet of their returns. The surprising thing is these superstars, with the exception of Buffett himself, lagged the S&P 500 in about 30 to 40 percent of the years studied. John Templeton, another legend—but not included in Buffett's study—lagged the big index about 40 percent of the time.

As Biggs writes: "None in the group always beat the S&P 500 probably because no one thought that was the primary objective." Even more interesting, some of the greats had relatively long periods of time, three or four consecutive years, where they lagged the market. "Almost invariably, sustained bursts of spectacular returns either preceded and/or followed those bad periods."[6]

An extreme example was Pacific Partners, which went through four straight years of lagging the market and five out of six. Yet, they had several years where they bagged returns of 120 percent, 114 percent, and

128 percent—so that, overall, they beat the market over 19 years by a wide margin: 23.6 percent per year, versus 7.0 percent for the market.

Many investors would not likely have stuck with them for the four years of wallowing behind the market. I can see the Morningstar reports now: "This firm has lagged the index . . . blah blah blah." Think what a mistake it would have been to get rid of Pacific then. Yet, that's what most investors are inclined to do. As Biggs writes, "Two or three straight years (much less four) of performance worse than the S&P 500 today would result in most investment managers getting fired. . . . People have short memories."[7]

If you think the professionals are any better at this, you'd be wrong. One of the striking things in reading Biggs's book is the number of times professional investors—people with hundreds of millions of dollars—buy near tops and sell near bottoms.

A money manager will have a good year and his fund will balloon from $50 million to $1.2 billion as money pours in. Then he has a bad year, and investors take their money out. The fund shrinks in half. Then he has a good year. . . . You get the idea. These are not just individuals making these decisions, but pension fund managers and people who handle multi-billion endowments. You would think they would be smarter about it.

Biggs notes the study done a few years ago by Dalbar, an investment research organization. Dalbar's study showed that the average mutual fund earned a return of 13.8 percent per year (during the great bull market that ended in 2000). Yet, the average investor earned only 7 percent per year. Why? Because the average investor was switching his money in and out at the worst times. He takes his money out when the market has a bad year and puts it back in when things are back up.

It seems clear from experience that beating the market every year is a pointless goal. It makes for an interesting record, but it's also clear you have to stretch out your time horizon and think long-term. That's how to get to the big gains, even though you may have to wander around in the darkness for stretches of time.

So there you have it, 15 funds to start with. You can always add your own.

Just in the first hunting ground you should have lots of names and possibilities. This one spot alone could keep you busy for a long time.

HUNTING GROUND #2: THE NET TANGIBLE ASSET VALUE SCREEN

The net tangible asset value (NTAV) screen is a proprietary screen I developed for *Capital & Crisis*, and it's had booming successes. It's my second-favorite spot. The basics of the screen are so simple that you could go to Yahoo! Finance and use its free screener. Just plug in the following criteria:

1. Market cap greater than $150 million (just to strain out the micro-caps)
2. Price-earnings ratio greater than 1 (gets rid of the companies losing money)
3. Price-to-book ratio less than 1
4. Debt-to-equity not to exceed 0.30

That's it. Then you get a list of names, maybe 15 to 25, depending on the market. Not too long, but long enough. Now you are ready to sort through them. Your first run-through could be to eliminate those companies whose net tangible assets—this number is available right off of Yahoo when you click on "Balance Sheet" and scroll down to "Net Tangible Assets"—is less than market cap. You do this because some companies have lots of goodwill and other soft assets that are not worth much. You want to exclude those.

You should have a short list of good candidates to consider. Many of these names will be scary. But don't be put off too easily. Look at these stocks individually and stick with those that have the best-looking balance sheets—lots of cash and little debt. Often these opportunities are worth betting on.

I issued a report to my readers, published on April 1, 2005, recommending five such stocks. One year later, these stocks were up an average of 87 percent. Two of them had more than doubled and every position was profitable, with the worst stock gaining 18 percent over that time.

A brief synopsis of the Fab Five:

- Arch Capital Group (NASDAQ: ACGL), an insurer and reinsurer, finished up 44 percent.

- Companhia Paranaense de Energia Copel (NYSE: ELP), a Brazilian utility relying on low-hydroelectric power, gained 115 percent.
- Industria Bachoco (NYSE: IBA), a Mexican producer of poultry, gained 17 percent.
- Imperial Sugar (NASDAQ: IPSU), a sugar refinery in Sugar Land, Texas, rose 211 percent.
- Presidential Life (NASDAQ: PLFE), a boring old life insurer, rose 60 percent.

Again, the NTAV screen is rich in possibilities. You will find among these stocks many unknown names. Yet many of them will prove bargains. I've used this screen to good effect, and it is so simple that you should give it a look, too.

Sometimes it won't give you any good names. That's okay. That's why we have more than one hunting ground. It may be months and months before a fat buffalo wanders onto your land. In the meantime, keep looking.

HUNTING GROUND #3: THE VALUE LINE INVESTMENT SURVEY

The Value Line Investment Survey contains a wealth of information. It's a great place to go to get a quick financial snapshot of a company. The folks at Value Line also put together some useful screens, which I frequent to search for names.

For example, I like to peruse the screen for stocks with the widest discounts-to-book value. A lot of the stocks on the top of the list— with the widest discounts—are pretty junky and scary. But as you work your way down the list, some interesting names and some good businesses pop up.

Keep an eye on that list. Just be careful. Continue to apply the same kind of analysis and thinking offered up in the earlier chapters of this book—think about enterprise value and cash flow and look for financial strength. You'll wind up passing on 95 percent of the names on this list—but the handful that pass muster will be well worth the effort.

Another good one is the screen for "bargain basement" stocks.

This screen looks at price-earnings multiples and price-to-new working capital ratios that are in the bottom of the Value Line universe—implying they are cheap. Usually the list is pretty short, and you can get a quick glance at what's unpopular in the market.

There is often some good stuff here. The best thing about these screens is that you can just go to your local library once a week and check them out if you don't want to subscribe to the service.

It doesn't get much more economical than that.

Again, it's just another reliable place you can turn to for a good list to research—a sort of sifter that makes your job easier.

HUNTING GROUND #4: SPIN-OFFS AND OTHER SPECIAL SITUATIONS

Another favorite of mine is spin-offs, which continue to be a rich source of ideas even though the idea itself seems to be well covered and known. For example, in March 2006, *Barron's* ran a cover piece on spin-offs. There were 27 spin-offs in 2005, and nearly every one was a solid winner. Every year there is a piece on how great spin-offs are, but no one seems to catch on.

Anyway, for more on spin-offs, read on.

The Best Investments Are the Ones They Give Away

In 1900 Frederick Weyerhaeuser acquired a block of 900,000 acres of timberland from the Northern Pacific Railroad for the paltry sum of $6 per acre. The Northern Pacific didn't particularly care about this timberland and didn't know the market for timber. After all, Northern Pacific was in the railroad business. It obtained the timberland on the cheap from the government, and when it didn't need the land for its railroad, it sold it.

Weyerhaeuser, on the other hand, was America's "Lumber King." He knew a good stand of trees when he saw it, and he appreciated the value of timberlands, having worked in mills since he was a youth. Over the years, he had accumulated a fortune in timberland. At the time of Weyerhaeuser's purchase from Northern Pacific, the acreage under his control was the second-largest such holding in the United

States. At the time of his death in 1914, his fortune was estimated at over $300 million—and his timberlands were worth substantially more than $6 per acre.

Savvy buyer. Indifferent seller. Result: a great investment opportunity.

One way to think about investing is to look for indifferent sellers. Examples include small-capitalization stocks, obscure or illiquid securities, and unique situations—such as spin-offs, divestitures, merger securities, rights offerings, restructurings, and a host of other lesser-known and underfollowed situations.

If you don't know what these things are, don't worry. I'm going to explain in this section one of the best places for individual investors to look for bargains.

These special situations, as they are often called, have traditionally been the province of some of the greatest investors. These were the kind of rich veins that the young Warren Buffett routinely mined. During his time running the Buffett Partnership (1957–1969), before Berkshire Hathaway, there were some years in which special situations made up more than half of his profits.

Of course, Buffett was not the only one dining off the tasty menu in the bistro of special situations. Other sharp-eyed value investors saw the same thing and made it a regular part of their investing diets, and they also enjoyed brilliant success.

Here's the story of one of them.

Gotham Capital: Turning $1 into $51.97 Ten Years Later

In 1985 a man named Joel Greenblatt started the private investment partnership Gotham Capital. Greenblatt made it his bread and butter to work in the special situations arena. He writes about his experiences in his book *You Can Be a Stock Market Genius*, which, despite its moronic title, is a serious treatment of investing and contains a lot of good advice.

Much of the book consists of case studies in which Greenblatt shows you how various spin-offs unfolded—Host Marriott from Marriott International, Strattec Security from Briggs & Stratton, American Express from Lehman Brothers, Liberty Media from Tele-Communications Inc. (which netted investors 10 times their initial investment in less than two years), and many others. Each of these experiences teaches us something about investing, in particular about the nature of special situations.

Greenblatt enjoyed tremendous success at Gotham Capital. Every dollar invested in the partnership when it was started in 1985 returned $51.97 by the end of 1994, for an annualized return of 50 percent. Just think— $1,000 invested in Gotham in 1985 returned $51,970 only 10 years later. In January 1995, all capital was returned to the outside limited partners.

While Greenblatt invested in a host of special situations, spin-offs were his favorite play. Why were spin-offs so appealing to Greenblatt and his merry band at Gotham? A little research shows that they had found a crack in the sidewalk of Wall Street that market-beating investments often slipped through.

Spin-offs Beat the Competition

Greenblatt points to a Penn State study published in 1993 that found that spin-offs beat their industry peers and outperformed the S&P 500 index by about 10 percent per year in their first three years of existence. That is a large margin of outperformance, but it's also no anomaly. A McKinsey & Company study also found that spin-offs produced returns in the first two years of independence of more than 27 percent annualized. Far from being only a U.S. phenomenon, the same spin-off outperformance occurs in other markets. A UBS study of European equities found that spin-offs substantially outperformed in their first few years of independence.

These studies looked at all spin-offs available in the market. The individual investor has the advantage of selectivity. We don't have to buy every spin-off, nor do we have to pick them randomly. Assuming the investor can cherry-pick the lot and avoid the dogs, there is a good chance to do even better.

You would think that the market would adjust and chip away at those outsized returns. Spin-off outperformance is a well-known phenomenon, documented and studied. If investors were to bid up the shares of spin-offs, the outperformance would disappear over time. But as Greenblatt and others have pointed out, there are good reasons why the well of promising spin-off opportunities will continue to be refreshed on a regular basis.

Before I tackle the reasons for this apparent inefficiency, let us consider the various reasons why companies engage in spin-offs at all:

- *To spin off an unrelated business.* Big unwieldy conglomerates that are involved in everything from insurance to restaurants may decide to separate an unrelated business to unlock the value in that business.
- *To separate a "bad" business from a "good" business.* Sometimes a company with a profitable core of operations will spin off a laggard that is draining resources and management attention from the main group. Once separated, each of the businesses can stand on its own merits, often to the benefit of all.
- *To unload debt or other liabilities.* Sometimes a spin-off will be loaded up with debt, freeing the parent company but leaving an overleveraged business in its wake. The spin-offs that have failed have often been of this kind. However, this maneuver can be lucrative for the parent company, as you might imagine.
- *To take advantage of tax benefits.* A spin-off can qualify as a tax-free event and may be the most efficient way to pass value on to shareholders. If the company were sold outright, for example, the cash distributed to shareholders would be taxable.

There are sound economic reasons for spin-offs, and this may explain their initial outperformance. Think about it: You have a new company with a new, dedicated management team that is likely to be highly motivated. As Greenblatt writes, "Pent-up entrepreneurial forces are unleashed. The combination of accountability, responsibility and more direct incentives take their natural course."[8] Curiously enough, as Greenblatt points out, the biggest gains from spin-offs often come in the second year, not the first. This indicates that it may take some time for the changes to kick in and deliver tangible results.

Okay, so we've seen some evidence on spin-off outperformance, and we know the motivation behind spin-offs and why they happen. All of this makes good sense. So why does Wall Street continue to ignore this apparent low-hanging fruit? There are good reasons for that, too.

Why Wall Street Misses Spin-Offs

The first reason is simply that Wall Street and the big institutions don't want spin-offs. They are often too small to make a difference. If you own shares in a big company and you are getting some small distribution of shares in a spin-off, it's easier for you just to sell the shares rather than dedicate any resources to try to figure it out. Again, the spin-off is too small to worry about.

Plus, if you invested in an insurance company and suddenly this insurance company is spinning off its smaller credit card operation, do you get excited? You're not interested in credit cards—you're interested in the insurance company. As Greenblatt notes, "Generally, the new spinoff stock isn't sold, it's given to shareholders who, for the most part, were investing in the parent company's business. Therefore, once the spinoff shares are distributed to the parent company's shareholders, they are typically sold immediately without regard to price or fundamental value."[9]

This usually creates selling pressure on new spin-off shares as institutions unload their stock. Since many spin-offs are small, they have little, if any, analyst coverage. And a freshly minted spin-off is not likely to be an immediate user of Wall Street's services. In other words, it doesn't have investment banking needs, so Wall Street is not likely to be interested in promoting the stock. There is little or no hype surrounding its shares. In fact, management may have an incentive to "talk down" the spin-off, since their incentive stock options are priced at the initial market price of the spin-off shares. In this case, it is in their best interest to start at a low price, then talk it up and promote it later—sometimes months later.

As Greenblatt says, the inefficiencies in the spin-off market are "practically built in the system" and should continue. Knowing this, how can we take advantage of spin-offs?

Greenblatt points to three characteristics of a winning spin-off:

1. Institutions don't want it (for reasons such as those discussed here). Sometimes very large companies spin off companies that are still quite large and attract a lot of attention. Investors are likely to find the buried treasure in smaller companies.
2. Insiders want the spin-off.
3. A previously hidden investment opportunity is uncovered by the spin-off transaction.

If you can capture a couple of these, or even one of them, you stand a good chance of having found a potential spin-off winner—and outperforming the market by 10 percent or more. Heck, you could do a lot better than that if recent history is any guide.

How to Find Spin-Offs

There is no easy way to find spin-offs. You just have to read the *Wall Street Journal, Barron's*, or some financial pub and keep your eyes peeled for any mention of spin-offs. You're not going to find oodles of them. They come in spurts. Some years you may get only a dozen, and in other years there may be 30. And you won't be interested in *all* of them. But again, we're talking about hunting grounds, and spin-offs are definitely a great source of ideas to research. Even if you invest in only a couple of them, the results will make it well worth your while.

If you want to cheat, there's a guy named Stewart Whitman who regularly posts all spin-off activity at http://www.siliconinvestor.com. It's a great message board, and I'd encourage you to visit.

Another way to cheat is to follow the Claymore/Clear Spin-Off (CSD) Exchange Traded Fund (ETF). An ETF is like a mutual fund. The Claymore/Clear Spin-Off ETF tracks spin-offs. You can look up this ETF, under the ticker CSD, and see what it holds. Or you can go to www.claymore.com and look at the fund's holdings. So there's your list of spin-offs to start researching. If you're really lazy, you can just buy the fund.

One of the more successful spin-offs I recommended recently was Ameriprise.

The stock only started trading on September 30, 2005. It was spun out of American Express, with investors receiving one share of the new company for every five shares of American Express they owned.

Wall Street hated the stock. Of the 13 analysts who followed the company, there were nine holds and one sell. That's terrible sentiment in an environment where analysts still hand out buy recommendations like doughnuts—by the dozen.

Wall Street analysts didn't like Ameriprise's management, which has remained somewhat reticent. Plus, the CEO was shy and a terrible speaker.

But the company was nonpromotional for good reason. Its incentive stock option plan was not set yet. When it was priced, they would start to talk. But in the beginning they had every incentive to lay low and keep the stock price low as well.

This is not uncommon in the spin-off arena, and it's one of the reasons spin-offs tend to do well.

A year later, Ameriprise was up 65 percent.

Cater to the "Mass Affluent"

Ameriprise (NYSE: AMP), formerly American Express Financial Advisers, is a large established player in its markets, with the fifth-largest sales force in the United States (over 12,000 financial planners). In addition, the company counts over 2.8 million clients and owned or managed over $410 billion in assets.

The company caters to what it calls the "mass affluent," a demographic slice that controls 50 percent of the nation's investable assets, is growing two times faster than market, and has an acute need for retirement products.

But the reason to get excited about AMP has more to do with its potential transformation now that it's independent—a card that AMP can play and that others don't have.

There is something to be said for the freedom of being independent. As part of American Express, Ameriprise didn't get a lot of attention. As evidence of this, consider that the company has paid out $2.8 billion in dividends since 2000. This represents a high 77 percent payout—money that could have been used to grow the business.

The company also had a marketing budget of $30 million before it was spun off. The budget for 2006 calls for spending $300 million on marketing. And all that advertising will bring in additional sales.

The real interesting part of the separation is that American Express infused Ameriprise with an additional $1.1 billion in cash before the spin-off. This is sort of like a parent's parting gift to junior to help him make his way in the world.

Cash-Rich and a Clean Book

This $1.1 billion made Ameriprise overcapitalized. As of the third quarter of 2005, Ameriprise had $2.6 billion in cash, or nearly one-third of its market cap. That's a lot of cash, and it represents an impressive war chest for the company to use to grow and expand the business.

Its debt load is already much less than that of peers, and its intangible assets as a percentage of assets are the lowest among its peer group.

This gives the company a pretty hard book value relative to its peers. A life insurance company generally trades at book value if there is some question about the quality of that book value or if the company's return on equity (ROE) is poor. Neither of these conditions is found at AMP. As we've seen, the book value is pretty good, and the ROE looked low only on the surface: all that cash had the effect of depressing the company's return on equity. Essentially $1.1 billion was added to the "E" in ROE before "R" had time to catch up.

Based on adjusted ROE numbers and the quality of the book, I put AMP at a $65 value—75 percent above the market price at the time. In the meantime, book value was about $31 to $32. So our downside was low. These are exactly the kinds of investments I look for: lots of upside potential, with limited downside risk. I told readers to look at a two- to three-year holding period to give the transformation time to take hold.

Again, spin-offs are a great source of investment ideas.

HUNTING GROUND #5: GREENBLATT'S "MAGIC FORMULA"

You have probably already gathered that Joel Greenblatt is one of my favorites. Greenblatt is one of the all-time greats, even though, strangely, he is not all that well known among casual investors. Certainly, his fame is nowhere near Warren Buffett's or even Peter Lynch's. Yet his record speaks for itself. Clearly, he is a man worth listening to.

I've mentioned his first good book on investing, titled *You Can Be a Stock Market Genius*. Despite its clownish title, this was an important contribution to the investment literature, as it dealt with special situations—such as spin-offs—and showed how and why such investments often work out. It fleshed out and brought to a wider audience a set of strategic options previously known only by Wall Street insiders and certain enthusiasts.

Well, Greenblatt has done it again, this time in a new book titled *The Little Book That Beats the Market*. In it, Greenblatt divulges his "magic formula"—a strategy that, over the last 17 years, has returned 30.8 percent versus only 12.4 percent for the S&P 500 over that time.

The basic goal of Greenblatt's screen is to *find good companies at bargain prices*. To do that, Greenblatt relies on two simple clues—and both are concepts that have been used by value-minded investors for decades.

Two Simple Clues to Stock Market Success

Those two simple clues are really just two ratios. All of the inputs are readily available on a company's financial statements. The first is *return on invested capital* (ROIC) and the second is *earnings yield* (EY).

The first is a measure of quality. When comparing businesses, all other things being equal, the higher the return on invested capital the better. Let's forget about stocks for a minute and just think about a very simple business. Think of invested capital as the amount of money you have to invest in the business. If you own a store and it requires $10,000 of your own money to open and returns $1,000 to you annually in profits, then you have a ROIC of 10 percent.

It's probably pretty intuitive that a higher number is better, right? If you make $1,500 annually, your ROIC would be 15 percent. More return for the same number of dollars invested. If a friend of yours has to invest $13,000 in his business to get the same $1,500, then his ROIC would be 11.5 percent. All other things being equal, you've got the better business (15 percent ROIC versus 11.5 percent).

So that's the first measure. Greenblatt puts his screen to the thousands of stocks on the market today and ranks them, highest to lowest.

But that's not all. This first test measures quality. We need something else to measure cheapness. We all know Microsoft or Wal-Mart is a great business, but is it cheap? Just because a business is great doesn't mean its stock price will rise.

That's where earnings yield comes in. The basic idea is to compare what a business earns to what its price is in the market (enterprise value). Enterprise value is the market cap of the stock less cash plus debt. Basically, it's how much, in theory, you'd have to pay to buy the whole company at current market prices. Therefore, the higher the EY the better. It means more earnings for your dollar.

It's like a more comprehensive price-earnings ratio turned upside down. A business with a 25 percent earnings yield is like a company with a price-earnings ratio of 4 (earnings yield equals one-quarter, or 25 percent). This is overly simplistic, because in Greenblatt's formula we're making a number of adjustments to both the "P" and the "E" in the price-earnings ratio. But it may help you understand the idea better if you think of it this way. Obviously, a price-earnings ratio of 4 is pretty darn cheap—and that's really what I'm getting at.

The formulas themselves are in the book, and I won't rehash them here. For the purposes of this discussion, the basic concepts are more important than the actual formulas.

Greenblatt's magic formula takes these two ratios, ROIC and EY, and screens thousands of stocks, ranking them from highest to lowest. The idea is that you should stick to buying good companies (ones that have a high return on capital). And you also want to buy those companies only at bargain prices (at prices that give you a high earnings yield).

As noted earlier, Greenblatt's magic formula stocks returned 30.8 percent over the past 17 years compared to 12.4 percent for the market. This is a remarkable result. Greenblatt has added yet another tool to the investor's toolkit.

Why It Works Now . . . and Why It Will Work Again

It is proof of a bad cause when it is applauded by the mob.

—Seneca

Ideally, a formula of any sort has to make sense intuitively and economically—such as Graham's net-nets and Greenblatt's ROIC and EY combination. These formulas are rooted in basic financial ideas that no one will refute. It's not like betting on some odd chart pattern or abstract macro theory.

And ideally, such a formula should be hard to stick with all the time. Otherwise, everyone would use it and the profits would soon disappear.

Graham's net-net idea was like that. Most of the net-nets were troubled companies. Investors hated these companies, which is why they were trading where they were. And it's also why the formula was able to work. It goes against human nature. People read it, they understand it, but they can't follow it.

Like those trying to follow the tenets of a religion, the vast majority of investors find that there are just too many other temptations and they are unable to stay on the righteous path.

It's the same with Greenblatt's formula. A lot of the companies you'll find on the list are not popular names, and indeed many of them have short-term clouds hanging over their heads. This makes sense, since it explains why they are so cheap. Still, these are tough buys for the average investor.

And it requires patience to stick with Greenblatt's idea, something else the average investor doesn't have a lot of—and that's being charitable.

As Greenblatt readily notes, the magic formula doesn't work *every year*. There are times when it will lag the market. But this is a good thing, in a way, because such underperformance will tax most investors' patience, and they will abandon it before the idea really has a chance to work its magic.

If you're interested in learning more about Greenblatt's ideas, you can check out his book or visit magicformulainvesting.com. I use this screen to find interesting candidates for further research. You should, too.

HUNTING GROUND #6: INSIDER BUYING

Insider activity is an easy hunting ground because it's reported in the *Wall Street Journal* or in *Barron's*, which makes another list of names easy to compile. You just go to these sources, put the names there on your watch list, and start going through them.

There are plenty of studies on insider buying, and I'm not going to rehash them here. Suffice to say, when you have lots of important insiders—the president, the chief financial officer, and so on—all buying a stock, that is a *good* sign. After all, they buy their own stock with their own money only because they think the stock will go higher. Insiders sell for all kinds of reasons, but they buy for only that one. And when you consider how much of their livelihood is already tied up in their company's fortunes, they are really making a big bet when they reach into their own pockets.

Again, this is just another fertile hunting ground, and one you should add to your list of places to go when you are looking for names to research.

HUNTING GROUND #7: DISTRESSED INVESTING . . . OR HOW TO MAKE 13 TIMES YOUR MONEY IN BANKRUPT COMPANIES

You probably have a hard time believing anyone could do well investing in troubled companies, much less bankrupt ones. And even if you know that investing in troubled companies can be enormously profitable, you probably think it must be very risky. On the contrary, it's safer than most styles of investing—when done well.

I want to spend some time on this style of investing, which I'm betting not many of you are very familiar with. It has led to some huge gains—some of them right under our noses.

Take the story of Kmart, for example.

Once a giant among retailers, Kmart struggled to keep up with the likes of its more agile competitors, namely Wal–Mart and Target. Years of futile efforts finally brought the old retailing icon to its knees. In January 2002, Kmart became the largest retailer ever to file for bankruptcy.

Left for dead by most investors, there were a few savvy money managers who saw some life amid the wreckage. Martin Whitman, manager of the Third Avenue Value Fund, was one of them.

Whitman has a long history of investing in distressed companies, going back to the 1970s. In the 1980s, he found a pot of gold in the bankrupt securities of Anglo Energy (now Nabors Industries). Whitman's cost basis in Nabors is around 40 cents on a stock that today trades north of $60.

What did he see in Kmart as he stood in the rubble, like Marius contemplating the ruins of Carthage? For one thing, he saw a company with $25 billion in revenues selling in the market for about $1 billion. Plus, Kmart owned a lot of real estate. There was a margin of safety—the risk of loss, he estimated, was low and the potential profit was enormous.

So he bought some of the company's debt for pennies on the dollar.

Bankruptcy's uncertain healing process began to take its course. (And it is highly uncertain, since it doesn't always work out. Sometimes the poisons that put the company into bankruptcy in the first place have no antidote.) The reorganization put thousands of employees out of work, closed hundreds of stores, and wiped out shareholders. The company belonged to its creditors—to people like Whitman. The survival of the company was in doubt.

But eventually Kmart emerged from bankruptcy. Much of the debt converted to new stock (the old stock was obliterated), leaving the new, postbankruptcy Kmart free of its heavy debt load. Not long after emerging from bankruptcy, Kmart and Sears agreed to merge, creating Sears Holdings.

Whitman made a 13-fold return on his investment in Kmart in about three years, though he still owns a large stake in Sears Holdings.

The question is this: *How could so large an opportunity—involving such a large and well-known public company—escape notice?* And is there a way for the individual investor to participate in investing in distressed companies?

In this section, we'll take a look at the secret world of vulture investing, or "distressed investing," if you prefer.

A Compelling Irony: Investing in Troubled Companies Lowers Risk and Increases Returns

The investing world is full of ironies, just as an old barn is full of bats. For example, many newcomers to investing find it hard to swallow the idea that you can make a lot of money buying things nobody else seems to want. (Or conversely, they find it hard to resist the fatal urge to jump in and buy what everyone else is buying.) Yet it is a nugget of investing wisdom that proves itself time and time again.

Which leads us to buying bankrupt companies.

Most investors avoid them like they avoid dark alleys in the bad part of town. Investing in these situations is analytically complex. The securities are usually illiquid, and the process itself is highly uncertain and tedious. Few investors are willing, and even fewer are capable enough, to dredge through the muck.

Therein lies the opportunity—as well as the answer to how Whitman was able to find a 13-bagger in broad daylight. Seth Klarman, the astute and successful investor behind Baupost Group, covers investing in financially distressed and bankrupt companies in his book *Margin of Safety*.

"The popular media image of a bankrupt company is a rusting hulk of a factory viewed from beyond a padlocked gate," he writes.

> Although this is sometimes the unfortunate reality, far more often the bankrupt enterprise continues in business under court protection from its creditors. . . . [A] company that files for bankruptcy has usually reached rock bottom and in many cases begins to recover.[10]

The shelter of bankruptcy allows a company to get back into financial health. Once in bankruptcy, companies can void leases, nullify long-term contracts, and even terminate prior labor agreements. Prior debts are restructured or swapped for new stock in the reorganized company (the old stock is often wiped out). The new post-bankruptcy company frequently emerges as a low-cost competitor, since it has shed many of its prior high-cost commitments.

Plus, bankrupt companies frequently build up cash—another source of value. Bankrupt companies also usually have substantial net operating losses (NOLs) carryforwards, which result from prior losses. NOLs can be used to offset future taxable income—a valuable asset in any market.

As Klarman notes, "When properly implemented, troubled-company investing may entail less risk than traditional investing, yet offer significantly higher returns."[11] Yet not all is cakes and ale. As with any investment strategy, investing in troubled companies can lead to disastrous losses when done poorly.

So You Want to Be a Vulture Investor?

"Vulture investor" is the name given to those who invest in bankrupt companies, after the ugly black bird with a taste for carrion. These practitioners often object to this label, because it smears them with the image of being rapacious speculators. The euphemism for their reclusive art is "distressed investing." It can be obscenely profitable. It also has the benefit of being somewhat countercyclical—meaning that opportunities abound in times of trouble.

The problem for the individual investor is that these opportunities are usually out of reach and well beyond his circle of competence. (Or put another way, the average Joe doesn't know a thing about it.)

Maybe you're still a little skeptical about this "investing in bank-rupt companies" idea. Is this some newfangled idea, the latest fad in investing? Not at all. In fact, the idea has been around for a long time. Many a savvy value investor keeps a special arrow in his quiver for the opportunities provided in distressed companies.

Let's take a quick look at the deal that really put vultures on the map of the investing world.

Penn Central Goes Down

> *The information flows were very bad. Penn Central hadn't happened yet.*
> —*Michael Price, former money manager of the fabled Mutual Shares*

In an interview with Peter Tanous in *Investment Gurus*, Michael Price gave some perspective on distressed investing. Before Penn Central, people didn't realize how much money you could make investing in bankruptcies. It would take many more years before the secret got out. The process essentially creates cheap common stocks as old debt is swapped for new stock in the refurbished company.

When Penn Central went down, the secret was out.

The bankruptcy of the Penn Central Railroad in 1970 was a watershed event in the history of investing. It was the largest bank-ruptcy of its time—by far—with liabilities exceeding $3.6 billion. The dissolution of the railroad also created the largest opportunity for vultures, then a small group of investors who were little known outside of informed Wall Street circles. The staggering successes of these specialists in this case would lead to the creation of a number of imitators.

Penn Central, in addition to being a railroad, owned a collage of assets—undervalued real estate, untapped natural resources, and even amusement parks. Penn Central also had layers of debt, much of it secured by land, tunnels, and other property. This is what the vul-tures saw. They saw an opportunity to purchase the debt—for pen-nies on the dollar—backed by valuable assets available on the cheap.

Once the reorganization was completed, these vultures reaped gains that were multiples of their initial investment. Marty Whitman plunked down $100,000 for mortgages backed with loads of assets and made five times his money within a year.

Given its size, there were lots of players in the Penn Central bankruptcy. Goldman Sachs bought bonds for 13 cents on the dollar and eventually got back 100 cents on the dollar. Balfour Investors, another vulture group, bought its stake for 20 cents on the dollar and sold out for 78 cents only a few years later—having more than tripled its money.

In short, after Penn Central lots of investors discovered how profitable this "vulture" work could be.

A Taste for Carrion

Just like in nature, you need scavengers to clean up.
                                              —*John Stark, vulture investor*

Before Penn Central, distressed investing was truly a small cabal of practitioners. Modern-day vulture investing probably dates back to the rubble of the Great Depression. That's when the dean of vulture investing got started.

Max Heine, a German immigrant, had a passion for investing. According to Hilary Rosenberg in her indispensable book *The Vulture Investors*, "Heine took advantage of the gap he saw between the price of a bankrupt company's stocks and bonds and the value of that company's assets."[12] His guiding principle: Don't lose money.

Heine would prove an invaluable teacher to such modern investors as Michael Price and Seth Klarman (who dedicates his book *Margin of Safety* to the memory of Max Heine). I wish I had more information about Heine. He is a seminal figure, like a Ben Graham for vultures, yet there is little out there about him. I would bet that today's investors could learn a lot from Heine.

In the wake of Penn Central, the vultures would fan out into other arenas in the economy. The '70s recession created opportunities in real estate, particularly in distressed real estate investment trusts (REITs). In the 1980s, the vultures found fresh carrion in the remnants of the junk bond meltdown and nasty downturns in energy and steel that created a new crop of corporate wounded.

It's really a timeless strategy. As long as there are mistakes, recessions, bubbles, and busts, there will be carrion for vultures. The economy will continue to produce new failures, and each vintage will bring its own unique flavors.

Let's take a quick look at how bad times create opportunities for vultures.

The Magic Carpets of the 1980s Come Down to Earth

"The stock market crash of October 1987 sounded an alarm on the economy, and the collapse of the junk bond market two years later was the final bell: The economy was screeching to a halt," Rosenberg tells us. "Companies that had been taken private through junk bond–financed leveraged buyouts, the magic carpets of the 1980s, plunged to the ground."[13]

Let me hang a few numbers on this idea, and it will give you some appreciation for how bad times create opportunity for vultures. In 1988 corporate defaults totaled $4 billion, double what they were the prior year. In 1989 they doubled again. In 1990 they more than doubled yet again. By 1991 about one in ten junk bond issuers were in default, and bankruptcy filings surged to record highs. These were heady times to be a vulture investor.

Since the economy has been strong of late, the number of bankrupt companies has been dwindling. Plus, the proliferation of hedge funds has not helped the old vultures' cause. Hedge funds, starved for returns, have expanded and reached into new areas—such as investing in distressed companies.

Put those ingredients together—fewer opportunities plus more players involved—and you get a loaf of miserable returns. "Now is not a good time to invest in distressed securities," opines Barry Colvin, president of Tremont Capital.

As with the economy, the cycles in distressed investing will turn like all investment cycles do. The time to invest is when things have been bad, as has been the case for vultures. Get in then, and when the cycle changes, you'll be there to catch the wave.

That's the way I feel about distressed investing now. Yes, results have been poor for the last several years, but storm clouds can readily be made out in the distance. Rest assured that business cycles happen, even when people believe they no longer do.

One of the Best Distressed Investment Firms in the World

It has been called many things—a conglomerate, an investment holding company, a younger, smaller version of Berkshire Hathaway.

To some, however, it is simply the best distressed investment firm in the world. This latter view is most apt in my mind.

Leucadia National (NYSE: LUK) has been around a long time. Since 1978, the company has compounded its equity at a 20 percent annual clip. Every dollar invested in Leucadia in 1978 turned into over $900 today—a track record that lays waste to the return on the S&P 500 over that span, beating it 16-fold.

Leucadia buys assets that are out of favor and cheap, often in bankruptcy, and then it works to rehabilitate the company. Basically, Leucadia is a vulture.

Lately, though, the results have not been so stellar. Ian Cumming and Joseph Steinberg, chairman and president, respectively, readily concede that their results over the past two years have not been good.

Their accounting for this in their annual letter is insightful. First, they recall a similar time in the late 1990s when there was a tremendous increase in asset prices. Leucadia sold many of its holdings at that time for huge gains—sales that, in retrospect, look brilliant.

Messrs. Cumming and Steinberg note the competition from "35-year-old hedge fund managers—private equity firms who have never known a bear market—and other investors willing to invest at high prices in risky assets with seemingly cheap money." They call them "unguided optimists."[14]

The Leucadians, too, cite their own reasons for optimism about the future. They note that of the dozen or so companies that still maintain AAA–investment grade ratings, four are under investigation for alleged financial mischief. In discussions with a bank chief, Cumming and Steinberg relate how the banker "allowed that many deals will likely blow up." "While we thank the banking community for creating future inventory for future investments," they write, "it is difficult to remain disciplined and on the sidelines in a game we love."[15]

Leucadia sits on a pile of cash: about $1.6 billion ready for future investment, as I write. As Cumming and Steinberg say, their investment philosophy is "bimodal": either they invest in high–return opportunities or they sit on the sidelines. There are few better ways to play the turn in the credit cycle than to shack up with Leucadia and its excess cash.

Leucadia relies on a handful of investment principles that stitch together the apparently unrelated investments that make up its portfolio.

These principles are often repeated in their annual letters (I've read them all going back to 1998):

1. Don't overpay.
2. Buy companies that make products and services that people need and want and that provide them as cheaply as possible with consistently high quality. Search out candidates in out-of-favor industries that have turnaround potential. Our record as midwives to resuscitating disorganized, unprofitable, bedridden, and moribund companies is pretty good.
3. Earnings sheltered by net operating loss carryforwards are more valuable than earnings that are taxed by the IRS.
4. Pay employees for performance and expect hard work and honesty in return.
5. Don't overpay.

This is a neat collection of simple but effective principles. Leucadia's disparate collection of businesses makes a lot of sense in the context of this investment philosophy.

A Throwback to the Way Business Used to Be

I also like the fact that Cumming and Steinberg own 25 percent of Leucadia between them. Compensation is modest, only $650,000 in salaries each last year—a drop from $1.8 million each in 2003. You hardly ever see that.

There was a time when it would have struck the investing public as absurd that a man would run a company without owning a big stake in the enterprise. This is a point made in Frederick Lewis Allen's *The Big Change*, a highly readable and entertaining look at sociological changes in American life, published in 1952. Allen discusses the radical change in corporate ownership:

> In 1900, capitalism was capitalism indeed. Businesses were run by their owners, the people who had put or had acquired the capital with which to finance them. . . . It would seem wildly irrational that a man should manage the destinies of a corporation while owning only a minute fraction of its stock, as so frequently happens today.[16]

Leucadia is also a bit of a throwback in this respect, in that management owns a good chunk of the enterprise. This should align their interests more with yours as a shareholder.

An investment in Leucadia is also a bet on the investment acumen of Cumming and Steinberg. Bearish commentators worry about succession plans, as Cumming and Steinberg are both in their late sixties, in much the same way people worry about replacements for Buffett and Munger. Fortunately, money management is a game that can be played late in life. Marty Whitman is still chugging along past his eighties, and Sir John Templeton is in his nineties. I think worries about succession are a bit premature in the case of Cumming and Steinberg.

Anyway, I love Leucadia as a long-term keeper stock, as long as Cumming and Steinberg are calling the shots. It's also a great way for the everyday investor to play the vulture market.

Otherwise, while I like the idea behind vulture investing, it's beyond the pale of most investors. I've added it on here only because so few investors seem aware of the money to be made in this area. Plus, you can keep your eyes out for companies coming out of bankruptcy and give them a good look. While you won't make the killer gains the vultures made in the bankruptcy process, you can still make massive gains, since most investors will likely shun a fresh bankruptcy graduate—giving you an opportunity to get the jump on the rest of the field.

HUNTING GROUND #8: THE EXPANDING PIZZA SLICES

One of the many funny stories involving Yogi Berra (some of which are surely apocryphal) goes like this: Yogi orders a pizza. Guy at the counter asks him: "Do you want it cut into four slices or eight?" Yogi responds, "Make it four. I'm not that hungry."

Of course, it doesn't matter how many slices you cut the pizza into. You still have the same amount of pizza. More slices simply means smaller slices. Investors take note. There are many people in finance still trying to make more pizza by cutting more slices.

Companies are like pizzas. And stocks are like pizza slices. If a company issues more shares, it is like taking the same size pizza and giving everyone a smaller slice of the pie. Most companies do this to some degree. They issue shares as compensation for employees and executives (usually via stock options). Or they just issue more shares to raise money, which they tend to blow—often on big acquisitions. I'm painting with a broad brush, but there's plenty of evidence to support the idea that most corporate managers are not particularly skilled investors of shareholder money.

However, there are companies that don't issue new shares. In fact, some of these companies repurchase shares from time to time, such that the number of shares outstanding *falls* over time. It's like sharing a pizza with fewer people. Suddenly, everybody's slice is a little bigger.

The key caveat here is simply that for this to work, the company's stock price should be cheap. You don't want management wasting shareholder money buying back its own shares if they are too pricey.

I've looked at share counts for a long time. All things being equal, I'd prefer to own the company that reduces its share count over the years. Increasing share counts means dilution of your investment, like someone slipping water into your beer. I think it's one of those things that most people don't think about or just ignore.

In fact, I think this idea could be a good stock screen—a tool you could use to screen thousands of stocks to come up with a short list you could research. According to our pizza slice theory, we look for stocks with falling share counts that are also cheap by some fundamental measure.

A Simple Market-Beating Strategy

Well, it turns out someone has already done the work on this. I read about it in James Montier's *Global Equity Strategy* report for November 2006, published by the investment bank Dresdner Kleinwort. He was citing a paper by Bali, Demirtas, and Hovakimian titled "Corporate Financing Activities and Contrarian Investment."[17] Okay, now that the boring attributions are over with, let's get to the juicy cuts.

Basically, they found that you can beat the market solidly with a simple value strategy: Buy the cheapest 20 percent (by price-to-book ratio) of the market whose shares outstanding are also falling. According to Bali et al., this would have given you a 5.5 percent edge per annum over the years they studied (1972 to 2002).

I used this simple insight to create a stock screen, using Morningstar's tools, to look for stocks that fit this picture. They had to be among

TABLE 4.2 Expanding Pizza Slices?

Stock	Price (October 3, 2007)	Ticker	Price/ Book Ratio	% Change in Shares
Nippon Telegraph & Telephone	$23.67	NTT	0.52	(11%)
AutoNation	$18.22	AN	0.98	(24%)
Westwood One	$ 2.96	WON	1.22	(18%)
Handleman	$ 2.90	HDL	27.00	(23%)

the 20 percent cheapest, using the price-to-book ratio as our rough proxy for cheapness. And they had to have a falling share count for the last five years. This was a tough screen, and only four stocks made the cut (as shown in Table 4.2).

I used five years to get the list down to a small number. You could use three years and get a lot more names—around 60.

It's also interesting to relax the share count requirement to simply those names whose shares outstanding don't rise. You get some interesting names this way, too. For one thing, the Mexican airport operator ASUR (NYSE: ASR), which I recommended in my newsletter, makes the list. So does the former *Capital & Crisis* holding Industrias Bachoco, which I tragically let go too early (it shot up 50 percent in the eight months after I sold it). Quality stuff abounds. Wesco is here, Charlie Munger's company, a solid long-term wealth creator. (Munger is Warren Buffett's right-hand man at Berkshire Hathaway.) Northwest Pipe (NASDAQ: NWPX), another company I recommended, was also one of the names generated by this more relaxed screen.

As I peruse the other names, I'm struck by the kinds of industries that keep coming up—transportation, insurance, various industrials, a paper company, a radio outfit, a furniture maker. There are few biotech stocks or tech stocks. There are not a lot of sexy names here.

I also flipped the screen around and tried to find the most *expensive* stocks by price-to-book and those with *rising* shares outstanding. The Bali paper showed how these stocks lagged versus the other group. Now, let's look at those stocks with rising share counts and high price-to-book ratios. Table 4.3 shows the top 10, sorted by market cap.

Ah, so here is where those sexy businesses wind up! Look at this list—a couple of wireless companies, a biotech company, a semiconductor

TABLE 4.3   Shrinking Pizza Slices?

Stock	Price (October 3, 2007)	Ticker	Price/ Book Ratio	% Change in Shares
China Mobile	$80.77	CHL	7.10	6%
eBay	$39.33	EBAY	4.63	24%
Gilead Sciences	$41.31	GILD	15.36	17%
Monsanto Co.	$84.24	MON	5.79	4%
Stryker	$71.79	SYK	6.13	928%
Broadcom	$36.26	BRCM	4.92	47%
ICICI Bank	$54.03	IBN	3.92	45%
Vimpel-Communications	$26.23	VIP	6.18	15%
Network Appliance	$26.33	NTAP	4.96	11%
Cameco	$41.67	CCJ	4.85	4%

company, eBay, and a uranium miner. There were 189 companies that made this screen—lots more than made the other screen.

As I peruse this list, I see lots of little biotech companies, risky tech stocks, some speculative mining shares, and other iffy propositions. In general, I'm struck by the differences in quality. Just a casual perusal of these lists would lead you to favor the first group—those with falling share counts.

All this makes intuitive sense, as any stock screen should. But one thing I like about this approach is that it incorporates the share count, which is something I've never seen in a stock screen before. As I said, this could be a useful screen when looking for new ideas.

The Bali paper provides solid evidence that companies that are net repurchasers of stock tend to make better investments than those that are net issuers of stock. Call it the "pizza slice theory of stock selection." It's just one other thing to think about when looking for worthwhile investments.

SUMMING UP: YOUR GENERAL GUIDE TO FINDING GREAT HUNTING GROUNDS

In addition to looking in all these places, I have some general hunting advice for you. In its most basic and boiled-down version it is this: Look for what's unloved. Ask yourself what the market is totally bored with. And don't be afraid to look abroad.

Let me tell you about one of my adventures in a particularly sleepy commodity that had a pretty good year in 2005 and the early part of 2006.

One fine morning in Paris, Jim Rogers met a French business writer for breakfast at a local hotel. Rogers, you'll recall, is the famous globetrotting investor who made a fortune running a hedge fund. He retired years ago at the age of 37. Now he travels around the world and writes books.

They chatted, perhaps over hot coffee and freshly baked croissants. The French writer, of course, was eager to discover what investments Rogers liked.

Rogers unwrapped a sugar cube and handed it to her. "Put this in your pocket and take it home," he advised, "because the price of sugar is going to go up five times in the next decade."

Sugar! She laughed, of course, looking at Rogers as if he were mad and skeptically gazing at the little white cube. The year was 2004. Sugar was then only about 5.5 cents per pound. No one was paying attention to sugar.

The beauty of the story, retold in Rogers's book *Hot Commodities*, is that he was right.[18] And his prediction looks to come true early, as you can see in Figure 4.1.

Since Rogers's prediction, sugar went up threefold, hitting 17.21 cents—the highest level in 24 years. That's a better performance than oil, or gold, or a lot of other commodities.

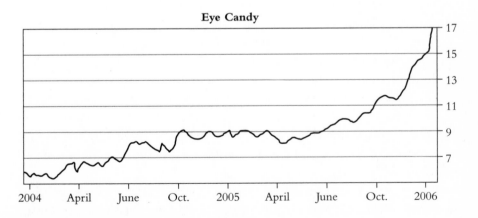

FIGURE 4.1 Eye Candy: Sugar Makes New Highs

Reprinted from Chris Mayer, "Profits Sweet as Sugar," *Capital & Crisis*, no. 25 (March 2006).

Sugar has had some great runs in the past. It soared 45-fold from 1966 to 1974, when it hit a record of 66.5 cents.

In his book, Rogers lays out a compelling scenario of tight supplies and growing demand. The biggest part of the argument involves Brazil, the world's largest producer and exporter of sugar. The pieces of his argument all came together, with new wrinkles that he could not have imagined.

Brazil uses part of its sugar output for ethanol, more so when the price of gasoline is high. That sort of shift has a big impact on the sugar markets as ethanol production consumes more and more sugar. Current forecasts hold that about 80 percent of Brazil's output will wind up in Brazilian cars.

That's one part of the demand equation. But there's more. The human race has quite a sweet tooth. Not only is there increasing demand for sweets in Western markets, but there is also steady demand from places like India (the world's largest consumer of sugar), Pakistan, Russia, and China.

Finally, there is significant demand for sugar from investment funds built to deliver returns based on commodity indexes. These funds have become more popular in recent years with the strong performance of many commodities. As a result, billions poured into the sweetener.

These are the pieces of the story Rogers figured out. All of this bodes well for demand. But there are supply constraints as well, some stemming from events he could not have predicted—like the worst hurricane season on record.

Hurricanes rolled over the Gulf Coast, damaging refineries in Louisiana and destroying sugar cane fields. The storms devastated crops in South Florida, too. As a result, the United States is importing more sugar to make up for the shortfall in domestic production.

Adding to the tight supplies is a dramatic production decline in Thailand, one of the world's bigger exporters of sugar. That country is experiencing a real sugar shortage. According to Reuters: "The shortage is so great in Thailand, where first drought and then flooding decimated the harvest, the government has capped prices and is threatening to jail hoarders."

China, too, has experienced bad weather that dropped production to a three-year low and prompted the government to sell sugar from stockpiled sources.

Europe won't make up the shortfall, because the 25-member EU must comply with a recent edict from the World Trade Organization limiting exports of sugar. It's absurd, but true. This, of course, delights sugar producers.

All of these factors drove sugar prices to new highs and put the squeeze on companies like Kellogg's and Coca-Cola. More than one-fifth of all sugar consumption is in the factories of cereal makers and bakers. Kellogg's shaved off a few cents from its earnings projections. Hershey, too, raised its prices on nonchocolate candies like Twizzlers and Jolly Rancher.

Many experts felt that if sugar supplies remained this tight, some refiners may have trouble finding sufficient raw sugar cane to process resulting in some food companies not having enough sweeteners for their products.

Ah, the refineries. The sugar refineries were also busy. In fact, most ran at full capacity. After years of listless performances, sugar stocks got hot. In April 2005, I recommended the shares of a small, sleepy sugar refinery, Imperial Sugar Company. With roots going back to 1843, it is one of the oldest companies in the state of Texas.

It was a cheap stock, trading for less than nine times earnings. Plus, the company had a strong financial condition. It had lots of cash, nearly $4 per share. For what was then a $14 stock, that was quite a bit. Imperial had virtually no debt. On an enterprise value basis, it was trading for less than three times its trailing EBITDA. Insiders were buying, too. Over the last six months prior to my recommendation, about 11 insiders bought $564,000 worth of stock. It was trading for only 80 percent of net tangible asset value.

If you followed my recommendation, you were up about 120 percent—in less than a year—including a substantial special dividend. Once again, it pays to look around in areas where people are not looking.

Now that you've got lots of places to look for names, you should have no trouble finding candidates to work on. In fact, you'll probably have lots more names than you know what to do with at first. That's okay, because once you start to work through them, you'll see the same names pop up often. After you've been doing this for a while and you've checked out a lot of names, each of these hunting grounds will yield only a few new names for you each quarter or month. It gets much more manageable over time.

When you start applying the principles and ideas of earlier chapters to these names, you are then well on your way to investing like a dealmaker.

CHAPTER 5

THE CRACKS AND CREVICES OF INVESTMENT WISDOM

Ain't only three things to gambling: knowing the 60–40 end of a proposition, money management, and knowing yourself.

—"Puggy" Pearson, the late, great poker pro

In 2002 famed money manager Bill Miller spoke to a roomful of students at Columbia Business School. Miller held them spellbound, expounding on investment ideas and concepts, sharing some hard-won wisdom. Asked at the end of the talk for any final advice, Miller quickly offered up an opinion.

The students expected perhaps some homage to the great Benjamin Graham, or some fawning words for Warren Buffett and Charlie Munger, or maybe even some encouragement to study the works of the great masters of the trade. That is not what they got.

Instead, Miller paid homage to a great poker player, Puggy Pearson, who died in April 2006.

Walter Clyde Pearson was born in 1929 in southern Kentucky before his family moved to the hills of Tennessee. The shape of his nose, said to have come from a fall at a construction site, earned him the name for which he would forever be known: "Puggy."

His father was a sharecropper and part-time whiskey bootlegger, which caused the family to lead something of a nomadic life. Before he was 10, Puggy had lived in 19 different places. He once quipped, "We were so poor that we had to move every time the rent came due."[1]

From such soils great gamblers are born. And he showed an early genius for cards. By the time he was 13, Puggy had hitchhiked his way to Tampa with only a few dollars in his pocket. A couple of weeks later he turned it into more than $1,000.

Jimmy the Greek, a prominent gambler of years long past, once said of Puggy: "Puggy's looks fool you, that pug nose and round face. . . . You can't conceive that a man like that is smart at anything."[2] But Puggy was a genius at the poker tables.

Puggy would go far and wide to find games. He had a large mobile home, and blazoned on the side in big letters was this quote: "I'll play any man from any land any game that he can name for any amount he can count." Smaller letters followed: "Provided that I like it."[3]

Does it seem odd to you that a great investor would invoke such a character as a source of wisdom before a blue-blood crowd at Columbia?

Believe it or not, investors can learn a lot from the greatest poker pros. Gambling isn't investing, but there are some similarities. Many of the best investors know this. I'm always amazed at the number of investors who play poker for exactly these reasons. John Templeton paid his way through college with his poker play, learning more about investing from poker than he did from school. Peter Lynch, the famed Fidelity stock picker, once said that every investor ought to take an undergraduate course in poker.

So Miller was actually in good company. What he did at Columbia that day was recite the Puggy quote at the top of this column.

Why? Knowing "the 60–40 end of a proposition" means knowing when the odds are in your favor. That's as fundamental as any investing process can be. "Money management" is about how much you invest. Do you put in 1 percent of your funds, or 5 percent or 10 percent? Money management is all about the structure and mechanics of your portfolio. And "knowing yourself" is all about understanding how you react to adverse circumstances. In his letter to shareholders, Miller went so far as to say: "I think if you understand what Puggy Pearson said about gambling . . . you'll know everything you need to know about investing."

Just goes to show how you can find investing wisdom in some out-of-the-way places. Yes, even in the thoughts of a poker great.

(As an aside, these old gamblers were great talkers. Puggy was on the receiving end of a pretty good barb at the 1973 World Series of Poker. He said to his opponent, "Amarillo Slim" Preston [from Texas]: "There wouldn't be no Texas if there wasn't a Tennessee." To which Slim shot back: "Well, if you folks could suck as well as you blow, we wouldn't need to be shipping no oil there."[4])

Puggy was a likable, laid-back fellow who was often found at the tables with a fat cigar between his teeth. Slim, a great poker player himself, regarded Puggy as the best all-around card player in the world.

And Puggy's three basics permeate the thinking of many great investors. Even though the market changes constantly, these basic ideas prove their usefulness in any market environment.

THE BASIC INGREDIENTS OF GOOD INVESTING

More Than You Know by Michael Mauboussin includes lots of interesting chapters on how markets behave and how investors behave in them. It uses a multidisciplinary approach, drawing on insights from biology, physics, psychology, and a variety of other disciplines.

Beyond this, it's loaded with fascinating stuff about how the market has changed over the years. Consider:

- The average lifetime of an S&P 500 company has dropped from 25 to 35 years in the 1950s to 10 to 15 years today.
- In the 1950s, the average turnover at a mutual fund was about 20 percent, meaning that the average mutual fund manager held on to his stocks for five years. Today that turnover ratio exceeds 100 percent—meaning that the average investor holds on to his stocks for less than one year.

It's a different market today. Things happen fast. Some of the higher turnover is a rational response to quickly changing market dynamics.

But most of it is just impatience and reflects the dominant speculative ethic.

Mauboussin also looks at those funds that beat the market over the decade ending in 2004. He finds that they share the following characteristics:

- *Low portfolio turnover.* "As a whole," Mauboussin writes, "this group of investors had about 27% turnover in 2004, which stands in stark contrast to turnover for all equity funds of 112%."[5]
- *Portfolio concentration.* Bigger bets. You're not likely to beat the market holding hundreds of stocks.
- *A value style.* "The vast majority of the above-market performers espouse an intrinsic-value investment approach," Mauboussin notes.[6] Paying attention to price pays. It seems so simple.
- *Geographic location.* This one was different. Basically, only a small fraction of these funds were located in East Coast financial hubs such as New York. Among the top locations: Omaha, Chicago, Salt Lake, Memphis, and Baltimore. I work out of my house in the suburbs of Washington, DC. The basic message: You have to break from the herd.
- *Limited time on macro forecasting.* When your primary focus is price to value, you can get a lot wrong on the big-picture side of things and still do very well.

I can't tell you how many times I come across these same elements in studying the most successful investors. These themes keep reappearing again and again. They are the basic ingredients of good investing.

There is much more to the book than what I've presented here. Take a look if you're interested. It will help you become a better investor.

Mauboussin also writes some good articles from time to time. In a recent piece titled "How Do You Compare?" he writes about how we think about and compare different investments.

One interesting idea he discusses is the notion of attribute-based versus circumstance-based thinking. It sounds academic, but it is really straightforward.

Some people select stocks based primarily on low price-to-earnings ratios. Or perhaps they look for high returns on equity or for stocks that have crossed their 200-day moving averages. These are examples of attribute-based thinking. Investors and traders are looking for specific characteristics.

By contrast, a circumstance-based investor thinks more in terms of context. For example, high price-to-earnings ratios may be okay in a certain circumstance—because of cyclically low earnings, for example. For a circumstance-based investor, the answer to the question of whether a low price-to-earnings ratio is desirable is always, "It depends." This investor focuses more on cause and effect and the individual situation at hand than on any numbers.

This latter type of thinking is more effective in markets, which are complex and ever-changing.

Here is a good quote from Mauboussin:

> Evolution provides a powerful argument for circumstance-based thinking. In evolution, species fitness—the ability to survive and reproduce—is not associated with specific attributes like size, color or strength. Rather, fitness relates much more to adaptability, which is inherently circumstantial. The parallel is clear: Attribute-based approaches work until the environment changes. When making comparisons in a dynamic environment, an attribute-based approach will let you down.[7]

Investing done right is inherently circumstance-based. There is no ratio or number you are aiming to find—no price-to-earnings ratio hurdles or growth rates or anything like that. Instead, you're looking for scenarios or circumstances in which things are happening that could make you some money. And these are often outside-of-the-box opportunities that mainstream investors would never consider because they lack the attributes these investors latch on to.

REALLY BIG WINNERS AND BIG FAT ZEROES

A few really big winners often make all the difference on your investment scorecard. To illustrate, let's take a look at an experiment by Murray Stahl, a creative essayist and money manager for Horizon Asset Management.

Stahl began his research when the last great bull market began: 1982. He put together a portfolio of six troubled companies in which few sane people would have invested: Chrysler, General Public Utilities (GPU), Pan American, Massey Ferguson, International Harvester, and White Motor.

Each of these stocks labored under mighty burdens. Chrysler's case is well known. White Motor shared the automaker's plight. General Public would suffer through the disaster of Three Mile Island. Pan American was a struggling airline. Massey and Harvester were farm equipment manufacturers suffering through the worst farm crisis since the Great Depression. Not a promising group, eh?

In fact, White Motor and Pan American ultimately cost investors everything—a big fat 100 percent loss on each. So, Stahl asked, how might this portfolio fare given that you know two of its holdings will go to zero?

The surprising answer is that it beat the S&P 500 over the ensuing 10 years—a 19.2 percent annual return versus 17.6 percent for the S&P 500. The success of Stahl's portfolio rested entirely on big home runs in Chrysler and GPU. Allowing these winners to run was the key. There was no rebalancing. So, at the end of the 10 years, Chrysler and GPU made up 93 percent of the portfolio.

Stahl concluded: "Thus, the arithmetic implication of success over a long period of time would be to possess an un-diversified portfolio. Yet professional investors are usually required to maintain a diversified portfolio at all times."[8]

The basic lesson behind Stahl's research is threefold:

1. Your investment results can depend on only a few really big winners. Stahl's experiment teaches us that a portfolio can suffer some grievous losses and still come out looking good. I've always preached avoiding the nasty big losses, but Stahl shows the arithmetic resilience of portfolio returns. Those really big winners cover even the worst sins—such as big fat zeroes.

2. And in order to have really big winners, you have to hold your winning stocks for a long, long time, which means . . .

3. You are not going to be able to maintain a fully diversified portfolio with lots of stocks. Because these winners will overtake

your laggards and assume an ever-larger share of your portfolio. Basically, expect to run a concentrated portfolio if you want to make big money in the stock market.

All of this implies low turnover in your portfolio. To illustrate another reason why low portfolio turnover can be good for your returns, let's turn again to brother Stahl, who relates an interesting story about the British war cabinet during World War II.

SEPTEMBER 1940: LESSONS FROM THE BRITISH WAR CABINET

The British war cabinet wanted to reduce the number of aircraft lost to mechanical failure. Ground crew inspected each fighter after 100 hours of flight time. The war cabinet thought that the number of mechanical errors would be lowest immediately after inspection and that the number would increase in linear fashion as flight time approached 100 hours. When they studied the issue, however, they found the opposite.

Inspections led to replacement of parts, which required some disassembly and reassembly of the aircraft. The more service on an aircraft—the more touches by well-meaning human hands—the greater the probability of error.

"The diligence of ground crews had the unintended consequence of increasing, not decreasing, aircraft malfunctions," Stahl concludes. So it is with investment portfolios. More moves mean more chances of error. "Intelligent inactivity is a rare virtue," Stahl writes.[9] In short, making a lot of moves in your portfolio gives you more opportunities to make a mistake.

In my personal investing and even in running my newsletter, there have been times when I thought I was smart in selling something, but it often turned out not to be the best decision. More often than not, it would have been better to just hold on.

If you do the upfront work well, picking good businesses and stuff you can hold for a while, then you can make time your ally. That's where we want to be. I don't always live up to it, but it's what I aspire to do.

MUHLENKAMP'S THREE-YEAR RULE

Ron Muhlenkamp runs the eponymous Muhlenkamp Fund, one of the best-performing mutual funds of the last 15 years. His recent book, *Harvesting Profits on Wall Street,* is a collection of essays he's written over the years.

Muhlenkamp believes investors should have a minimum time horizon of three years, which is long enough for the long-term dynamics of stocks to work in your favor. One thing he suggests you can do to cope with the dark and stormy nights: Don't price your portfolio so often.

He writes: "The bottom line is that if you price your portfolio every day, you are going to get huge volatility. If you price it once a week, you'll get less. If you price it once a quarter, you'll get less."[10] You get the idea.

Stocks bounce around a lot in the short term, and that can eat away at your nerves and your patience if you watch them every day. But over the longer term stock prices tend to follow value, and some of the volatility goes away. Most of it is gone after year three—hence Muhlenkamp's rule.

Worrying about your portfolio on even a monthly basis is like, in Muhlenkamp's words, "a farmer worrying about how much his crops grew in February."[11]

ADVICE MORE IMPORTANT THAN ANY STOCK PICK

Warren Buffett has said that no one should expect to find more than 20 gems in a lifetime of stock picking. That statement tells you a lot. Again—you can't be too active. Your big returns will come from a small number of stocks, and you have to sit on them to get the big gains.

Of course, most people don't want to just hang around waiting for perfect gems. Warren Buffett himself has made many more investments than his allotted 20—and he's made lots of mistakes along the way, like the rest of us.

Buffett has also said you have to be willing to sit through a 30 percent decline. The ability to hold on comes from having the right perspective on market prices. Price and value don't always move together. A stock can go down while the business still grows in value. Stocks can rise when the business is deteriorating. It happens all the time, and it is why we must divorce stock market price from underlying value.

Therefore, a decline of 20 to 30 percent is not usually something to get anxious about. We buy super-strong financial conditions. So even if they go down, we're confident they'll be back. However, there are limits. There's always a good reason if something drops 50 percent. Investors must walk a line. It is not easy, but it's the way great investors have made a lot of money in stocks.

The lessons here are worth more than a single stock pick. I recommend reading again, and thinking about, the insights from Stahl, Whitman, Muhlenkamp, and Buffett. They reinforce the good habits of investing.

IF YOU WANT TO OUTPERFORM THE MARKET

Another important lesson from studying the investment greats. . . .

Super-investor Anthony Bolton (more from him later) has said: "If you want to outperform other people, you have got to hold something different from other people. . . . [T]he one thing you mustn't hold is the market itself."[12]

This is a timeless bit of investment wisdom that the great investors all embrace. Yet in the mutual fund industry you find many "closet indexers." A closet indexer is someone who runs a mutual fund that is not an index fund and that does not bill itself as an index fund, yet to a large degree its portfolio matches an index (such as, say, the S&P 500).

So here you are, as a mutual fund investor, handing over your funds, presumably so that a human being will intelligently and thoughtfully manage them, yet many mutual funds barely escape being index funds. And you are paying extra for this, mind you. Actively managed funds charge much more in fees than index funds.

A pair of Yale professors created a statistic called the "active share" of a portfolio, which measures how much of a portfolio matches up against an index. If you have a portfolio that is essentially a replication, with minor modifications, of, say, the S&P 500, then your active share score will be low.

The measure also accounts for the weighting of your positions. So even if you own ExxonMobil, which accounts for 4 percent of the S&P 500, it could still raise your active share ratio if, for example, it makes up 9 percent of your fund. You get a high active share rating by doing two things: owning different stocks and owning different amounts of those stocks. Those who make big bets—like Bolton—would earn higher active share scores.

So-called closet indexers—those with scores between 20 and 60 percent—made up about one-third of all mutual funds in 2003, up from practically zero in the 1980s. In other words, it seems that stock picking is becoming a lost art. The trend is for more and more funds to largely mimic an index. Which brings up a question: Why invest with these people at all? You might as well shove your money in an index fund.

Well, not all fund managers have such low active share measures. In fact, most of the best investors have very high active share numbers. The Legg Mason Value Trust, run by Bill Miller, has an active share reading of 85 percent. That is a high ratio. Of course, Miller beat the S&P 500 for 15 straight years—though that streak ended in 2006. The Fidelity Low-Priced Stock Fund, another top performer, also had a high reading, 90 percent.

It's also interesting that the great money managers of the past had high active share ratios. Peter Lynch, when he was running the legendary Fidelity Magellan Fund in the 1980s, routinely had active share readings of between 70 and 90 percent.

Lynch is particularly interesting because a common criticism of him—even among those who are otherwise market-savvy—is that he had a big fund that "owned the market" and was fortunate to exist during a great bull market. The Yale study, however, indicates otherwise and confirms the conventional wisdom: Lynch was a great stock picker. (However, it is true that later in the decade the fund's active share readings plunged to around 55 percent as the fund ballooned and its performance lagged. Lynch left in 1990.)

Finally, the active share measure seems to have some predictive power. That is to say, those who have high active share readings tend to beat those who don't. Stock picking is a skill after all.

Some other funds with active share readings above 95 percent include the Brandywine Fund, Longleaf Partners, and CGM Focus— all with long track records of top performance.

All of this affirms the old wisdom: If you want to beat the market, you are going to have to own something other than the market.

MARTY WHITMAN—SAFE AND CHEAP INVESTING

Marty Whitman, manager of the Third Avenue Value Fund, is one of my favorite investors. After more than 50 years in this business, he's seen everything.

One of the best profiles of Whitman's approach comes from my favorite newsletter, *Grant's Interest Rate Observer.*

> The progenitor of the Third Avenue Funds is a man of settled views. On investment topics, he brooks no airy-fairy speculation. Once I made the mistake of asking him where he thought the stock market was going. His reply was silence. It was a forbidding, subfreezing silence, and the seconds it lasted seemed like hours. Something told me not to ask the follow-up question I had prepared about the likely course of interest rates.
>
> The precepts of safe and cheap investing, of which Marty is no doubt the master theorist-practitioner, sound deceptively simple. Insist on financial strength and honest management. (Marty, no utopian, actually gives you some slack on this criterion: he stipulates "reasonably" honest management.) Look for high-quality assets and nonburdensome liabilities. Seek out free cash flows from operations. Look for safety in the price you pay. Put not your trust in forecasts. Invest in what's in front of you. Don't shrink from investing in complex securities. Think two or three times before selling. Strive to understand the financial data under which an investor is fairly buried these days—that is, what the numbers mean, not just what they say.
>
> Marty doesn't claim that this is the one and only true church of investment. But that's the approach to investing that has worked for him and, of course, his fortunate investors.

It follows that the safe and cheap investor is a selective consumer of the news. He can afford to give the "A" section of the *Wall Street Journal* short shrift, he believes, because he is armored against macroeconomic or geopolitical disappointment. "Macro data such as predictions about general stock market averages, interest rates, the economy, consumer spending and so on are unimportant for safe and cheap investors, as long as the environment is characterized by relative political stability and an absence of violence in the streets," Marty has written. "The Whitmanian investor is protected by a margin of safety. The lower his cost basis in relation to net asset value of the company in which he invests, the less he stands to be buffeted by adverse news from Iraq, Iran, North Korea or even from Washington D.C."[13]

Whitman looks at investing so differently than others do. Wiley just republished his book *The Aggressive Conservative Investor* as part of its "Investment Classics" series. There is a lot to the book, but some of the insights are too good not to be highlighted here.

Early on, Whitman lets you know where he's coming from. "It has been our observation that the most successful activists have had much the same approach to investing that the most sophisticated creditors had toward lending."[14] As a former commercial lender, I know exactly where Whitman is going. Think safety first. Only after analyzing the potential loss does the safety-first investor look for profits.

But Whitman also makes the important point that lower risk does not mean lower profits. In fact, one thesis of his book is that lowering risks actually enhances your return. This is counter to conventional investment wisdom, which says you must take bigger risks to make more money.

Important insights fill the book, though I would caution you that it is not easy reading. Several points in particular stand out, and they are points I've emphasized in this book.

Companies create wealth in ways other than simply producing earnings, as I've discussed here. Businesses can own assets that appreciate in value over time; these gains are nontaxable and don't show up as earnings, yet they can be more important than earnings alone. A classic example is real estate companies, such as Orient-Express Hotels or Intrawest, which I recommended for well below the net asset value of the underlying properties, even though earnings were light at the time.

Focusing on assets can alert you to opportunities. But it can also warn you about pitfalls. Whitman uses the example of a bank stock trading for $12 per share and earning $1 per share on equity of $2 per share. For the asset-conscious investor, this would be a warning sign, since no bank can earn 50 percent on its capital for long. Clearly, this is a different conclusion than the one that would be reached by an investor focused on earnings. In Whitman's approach, the quality of assets is frequently more important than earnings.

Conversely, overcapitalized banks and financial institutions can be a source of value. Let's say that a $12 bank is earning 25 cents per share but has equity of $6 per share. On an earnings basis, it would look unattractive, trading for 48 times earnings. But the knowledge that banks typically earn 15 percent on equity, implying potential earnings of 90 cents per share, suddenly paints a different picture. The bank becomes a takeover target if it can't deploy its assets to bolster its earnings by expanding the business, buying stock, or making other strategic alternatives. If the bank can't do any of these things, someone else will relieve it of its cash.

The ability to finance long-term at super-attractive rates creates wealth. Whitman's focus on wealth creation also gives him rare insights into the value of corporate balance sheets. For example, he talks about how an office building in New York City financed with a 20-year mortgage at 5 percent when market rates were 9 percent has a valuable asset in its mortgage. If the mortgage loan is assumable, then a buyer would be willing to pay much more for the building with the mortgage than without. In this case, the company's books overstate the liability.

I would argue that few analysts consider this possibility in looking at businesses. One of my plays on this idea is Brookfield Asset Management (NYSE: BAM), which is able to finance dams and office buildings at long-term attractive rates. Nearly all of the companies I recommend enjoy strong finances and have access to capital at attractive rates.

I also love Whitman's emphasis on the fact that there are two distinct markets for stocks. There is the one quoted every day, and there is the market for control of whole companies. Frequently, there are differences between these two markets. "Thus," Whitman notes, "there is a long-term arbitrage that takes place because of the disparities between market prices and control values."[15]

When companies are too cheap in the publicly quoted market compared with the other market, control investors look to acquire shares. By acquiring shares, they can try to influence corporate policy or acquire control, with the idea of unlocking the value in the business.

Whitman's basic approach to investing is pretty simple, though it is much more difficult to practice. He has four points that essentially describe his strategy: buy companies that have (1) strong financial positions, (2) reasonably honest management, (3) the ability to make reasonable disclosures, and (4) buy at prices below estimated net asset value. Therefore, you only buy stocks that are "good enough, based on the four essential elements."

Whatever the market may throw at us—whatever interest rates do, whatever happens to the price of oil, whatever the state of the economy—paying attention to the basic details of corporate analysis provides "an anchor to windward." There is no aim for perfection. As Whitman says, "The primary motivation for purchases is that values are good enough."

RALPH WANGER—IN SEARCH OF ACORNS

Performance is a terrific differentiator, but it's hard to plan.
    —*Ralph Wanger, Columbia Wanger Asset Management*

It's rare that you open up a mutual fund manager's report to his shareholders and read about the Russo-Japanese War. But that's exactly the way Ralph Wanger opened his letter to Columbia Acorn Fund shareholders in 2005. "In May 1905," Wanger noted, "the untested Japanese Navy annihilated the Russian fleet at Tsushima. This was the first time a non-white country had beaten the main force of a European colonial power."[16]

That May was the 100th anniversary of that naval encounter. But that wasn't all. Wanger went on to discuss how a clerk at a German patent office, a non-academic who lacked a PhD, contributed three articles to the September 1905 journal *Annalen der Physik* that would each revolutionize its own branch of physics. The contributor's name was Albert Einstein.

Wanger dedicated the bulk of his letter to Einstein, admiring his achievements in what he called the "miracle year . . . a year of surprises." Little of his letter related directly to investing, which is, to say the least, unusual.

But then again, Wanger himself is not your typical investment thinker. From its launch in 1970 through 1996, his Acorn Fund—a small-cap fund that invests in fundamentally sound companies—gave shareholders an average annual return of 16.8 percent, besting the S&P 500's 13.1 percent return over that span. If there were a Hall of Fame for investors, Ralph Wanger would be a first-ballot shoo-in.

I traveled to Chicago to meet with the 70-year-old master. Today Wanger no longer actively manages money but acts as an adviser to the family of funds under the Columbia Acorn banner. I was not disappointed.

Wanger was witty, rolling off aphorisms as easily as if he were shucking corn. He was thoughtful and wise and exceedingly generous with his time (I was in his office for about two hours).[17]

I felt like a man who had journeyed to the mountain to meet with the wise sage on the meaning of life, given his, at times, cryptic responses.

"Do you still use themes to guide your investment decisions, as you discuss in your book?" I asked.

Wanger paused, thought for a few seconds, and then said, Yoda-like, "Themes are a result, not a cause." Before I could ask what he meant, he said, "I shall expound." And he did.

He talked about how the mutual fund business was the most competitive in the world and how hard it was to differentiate yourself among the many thousands of competitors.

Investment performance is one way, which led Wanger to deliver the statement quoted at the beginning of this section. One ingredient of good returns is holding down transaction costs and turnover, which can give you a significant edge.

Wanger had come to the conclusion that in order to minimize turnover, you have to hold stocks for a longer period of time. And in order to hold them for a longer period of time, you have to work with long-term themes and find companies you can live with for a while. In other words, you can't focus your attention on what's going to happen next quarter or next year (as most market participants do), but rather, you've got to look out further on the horizon.

Admittedly, it is not easy to do. But this is why long-term investing ought to work. As Wanger notes, if everyone is focusing on the short term, then long-term investing becomes an arbitrage between the long view and the short view. Working with themes is the result of making a decision to think long-term, avoid turnover, and lower transaction costs. That is what Wanger meant.

I complimented him on his book, *A Zebra in Lion Country,* and his newsletters, noting that few fund managers wrote like that. "Maybe Buffett," I said.

"He overwrites," Wanger opined. "Too flowery."

I mentioned Bill Miller at Legg Mason, whom Wanger complimented as an astute investor. Miller has beaten the S&P 500 for 13 straight years. However, as Wanger noted, if you had put your money in Acorn over that stretch, you would not have beaten the S&P 500 every year, but you would have enjoyed an average annual return one percentage point higher than Miller's.

"Hmmm," I said. "There is a lesson in that."

"There are several," Wanger responded. "Of course," he added with a wink and a chuckle, "I wouldn't have given you that information if we didn't beat him."

During Wanger's tenure at the head of Acorn, from 1970 to 2003, he averaged a robust 17.2 percent return. A mere $10,000 investment in 1970 was worth $174,059 by 1998. He handily beat the S&P 500 over that stretch and made his long-term shareholders rich. He is truly a legend in the industry.

I'll share some of the details of my interview with Wanger, including what many regard as the great secret to success in long-term investing. And I'll introduce a strategy for selling stocks that you can use for every stock in your portfolio.

Investment Insight #1: Stray from the Herd

Wanger has long been associated with small-cap investing. His 1997 book *A Zebra in Lion Country* illustrates the virtues of staying with smaller, lesser-known companies. He believes that the small-cap investor can get the jump on the big-money pros, whose main attention usually is with the large-cap stocks—where they can take big positions.

Wanger said that this may be less true now, and he believes there are striking bargains among some of the larger companies. This is because even with 50 to 60 analysts covering a stock, most, if not all, of them will be very close in their thinking about a company. Earnings estimates will usually be huddled together like frightened puppies.

With such a powerful collective mentality wrapped around a company, you might as well have only one or two analysts covering a stock. There is little independent thought in such an environment. And since the experts are wrong often enough, there is plenty of room for the sort of independent thinking that leads to profits.

"When everyone thinks alike," author Humphrey Neill liked to say, "everyone is likely to be wrong."[18] People often find this to be a counterintuitive conclusion, even those who have experience in financial markets. But much of the big money in investing has been made with uncommon or unpopular ideas that later bore fruit. On the other hand, buying what nearly everyone else is buying, or has already bought, has often led to some of the biggest losses. It is critical that an investor develop his own view of the world.

One way to think differently, Wanger advised, is to think longer-term. Shorter-term thinking dominates the investment world. I have written about this before in other places, but the idea is important enough to bear repeating. Proof of this short time horizon is provided in Michael Panzner's recent book, *The New Laws of the Stock Market Jungle,* in which he shows that the average holding period for an NYSE stock has fallen to a matter of months.[19] This is the culmination of a long trend. As recently as 1990, the average holding period exceeded two years; in 1975 it was over four years.

"This is why long-term investing ought to work," Wanger said. If most people are worried about the short term—say, the next quarter or two—then you can exploit that by buying stocks with temporary setbacks but solid longer-term prospects.

In a similar vein, investors can pay too much for bright-looking futures. "Growth fails because people cannot see the future," Wanger said. Reality frequently disappoints; dreams are often just dreams.

The basic metaphor behind Wanger's book is conveyed in the title. The zebra, to get at the best grass—the grass untrodden by the herd—must selectively stray from the safety of the herd. Investors must do the same.

Investment Insight #2: Know When to Sell

Wanger was just warming up. I had only asked for an hour of his time. But he would spend close to two hours with me. On the topic of when to sell, he had much to say. This is an area on which few investors dwell, professionals included. But Wanger articulated a bona fide strategy for deciding when to sell. It was the best advice on selling I have ever heard, and it is quite straightforward.

Wanger's advice was simply to make the reason you buy a stock "specific enough so you know when it is no longer true." That is, make it falsifiable or checkable. That way, you can keep checking back with your reason, and when it is no longer true, sell. Let me use a simple example to illustrate this powerful concept.

Say you buy a stock because you believe its business will turn around and you think it's capable of expanding its profit margins from 3 percent to 8 percent over the next five years. Newer, more profitable products are coming on board. The company has lagged competitors, but you've identified some catalysts that are going to change that. Whatever the reason, you pencil in "8 percent" and buy the stock.

Now you have a clear reason to sell. If the company doesn't meet your expectations, your original reason for buying the stock is no longer valid. Let's say that after year five the company's profit margin is only 6 percent. You were wrong, so you sell. It doesn't matter what the stock price did.

If, in year three, the company seems to be making progress, you hold on. Your original premise is still valid. It could still work out.

Conversely, the company may do much better than you expected. Maybe by year three its profit margins have gone to 10 percent. Well, you still sell. Once again, your reason no longer applies, so you should sell the stock.

Of course, you can revise and revisit your reasoning on a periodic basis. Just be sure to keep your reasons specific and checkable.

Many investors complain about how difficult it is to decide when to sell. Even the great ones do. Make it easy on yourself. Be specific as to why you bought it in the first place.

Investment Insight #3: The Stock Market Is a Loser's Game

Wanger emphasized this point intensely. In fact, he told me that if I do nothing but repeat this message in my newsletter every month, I would be doing my readers a great service. So what does it mean to call the stock market a loser's game?

It means that investors win only by exploiting the mistakes made by other investors. And this has profound effects on strategy—that is, on how an investor should approach the task of investing.

Charles Ellis's book *Winning the Loser's Game,* which Wanger recommended, elaborates the point. To illustrate, Ellis writes about the game of tennis. There are two games of tennis: the game played by the professionals and the game played by the amateurs.

The professional level is characterized by a great deal of skill and ability. Players hit the ball hard and usually where they want to. It becomes a strategic and tactical battle as well as an athletic contest. The professionals make very few mistakes. Theirs is a winner's game. The outcome depends to a great extent on the actions of the winners.

The amateurs, however, play a different game. There are few brilliant shots or long rallies. Far more balls are hit out of bounds or into the net. Errors are far more frequent. The winner is the one who makes fewer mistakes. Amateur tennis is a loser's game.

The way to win a loser's game is to make fewer mistakes. You play not to lose. So the advice for amateur tennis players is to worry less about powerful serves and to focus more on just getting the ball back over the net and keeping it in play.

THE GREAT SECRET OF LONG-TERM INVESTING

Ellis makes the case that investing is also a loser's game. Most mutual fund managers don't beat the market, and they don't beat the market because they make many mistakes. They buy and sell too frequently, for example, incurring excessive transaction costs. "To achieve superior or better-than-average results through active management," Ellis writes, "you depend directly on exploiting the mistakes and blunders of others."[20]

This means that the investors who make the fewest mistakes will be the winners. Investing is not about making explosive gains. It's more about avoiding losses. Investing is a defensive process. *The great secret of success in long-term investing is to avoid the serious losers*. That is the distilled, if unglamorous, wisdom that Wanger wanted to be sure I understood.

The essential task of the investor boils down to an exercise in managing risks. It requires patience and commitment to avoid the temptation of trying to hit home runs every time up. Always think about the possibility of losses and how to limit them. If you remember nothing else from this book, the idea of the market as a loser's game will serve you well over your investing career.

Investment Insight #4: Heed the Lessons of History

Wanger obviously loves history. His fourth-quarter letter to his shareholders opens with a short discussion of the Battle of Tsushima. This is followed by a much longer discourse on the achievements of Albert Einstein in 1905. He believes, with Patrick Henry, that we have but one lamp to guide us, and that is the lamp of experience.

This leads to another good metaphor from Ellis that is helpful in understanding how the stock market works. Think in terms of daily weather versus climate. The daily weather is short-term, while climate is a longer-term phenomenon.

The daily weather can vary significantly, and we can experience aberrations in it—such as cool days in midsummer or mild days in the dead of winter. But over the longer term, the bulk of the daily temperature changes fall into the general *historical* ranges for a geographic area. We can predict fairly reliably what winters will be like in New England and what summers will be like in Washington, based on history. The weather makes sense in the context of the longer-term climate.

When you invest, you should think about climates, not the daily weather. Ellis advises, "In choosing a climate in which to build a home, we would not be deflected by last week's weather. Similarly, in choosing a long-term investment program, you don't want to be deflected by temporary market conditions."[21]

To understand the stock market's "climates," the investor has to understand history. As Ellis notes, the more the investor understands how markets behaved in the past, the better equipped he will be to deal with the present and future.

There is a passage in *The Great Gatsby* that reminds me of this idea of mining the past for investment secrets. The narrator, Nick Carraway, writes about how he studied to become a bondman when he moved to New York:

> I bought a dozen volumes on banking and credit and investment securities, and they stood on my shelf in red and gold like new money from the mint, promising to unfold the shining secrets that only Midas and Morgan and Maecenas knew.

I love the way that reads. Investing may be one of the few disciplines in which mining the past is a practical exercise.

Investment Insight #5: People Get Paid for Doing Boring Things

People like big, sexy ideas. They love technology companies that look like they are going to remake the world. They are tickled by the promise of huge, rapidly growing markets. This is why semiconductor and biotech stocks are forever intriguing to most investors, despite the fact that they can be very erratic. They are like lottery tickets.

Yet, as Wanger said, people get paid for doing boring things. He mentioned that his firm owns some companies that do incredibly dull things. These included companies like Florida Rock Industries, which owns big gravel pits and sells sand, gravel, and crushed stone. Another was Wienerberger, an Austrian company that manufactures bricks and clay roofing tiles. Lots of companies that do very uninteresting things—like making window shades or door locks—get paid good money for doing it.

The main reason is that they have little competition. Money flows to the exciting, lottery-style companies. Few venture capitalists or entrepreneurs wake up and say, "Darn it! I'm going to open a gravel pit today." Entrepreneurial money and energy are largely attracted by the potential big payoffs in high-growth industries. Investors feed this phenomenon.

This leaves plenty of boring companies in boring industries that make a little extra profit margin, and their stocks can be good investments.

ROBERT OLSTEIN—STUDY THE BOOKS

There is a scene in *Moby-Dick* in which Ahab's second mate, Stubb, snookers French seamen out of a whale carcass. (Americans have always loved poking fun at the French, it seems. Published in 1851, the Frenchmen in Melville's grand novel are comical stereotypes.)

Stubb convinces the French that the dead whale is worthless. When the French leave it, Stubb retrieves the rich ambergris from the whale's intestines. Ambergris looks like "mottled old cheese" but is "worth a gold guinea an ounce to any druggist." Used in perfumes, cooking, candles, and more, the ambergris is a hidden treasure, passed over by most.

The Olstein Financial Alert Fund is a well-respected value fund now in its 10th year. The latest chairman's message reprints "The 10 Tenets We Live By."

They are interesting, if chock-full of investment jargon. For example, Olstein's first tenet is "We believe there is a high correlation between long-term performance and error avoidance."[22] In plainer English, this means: "We believe avoiding mistakes is the key to long-term investment success."

Particularly interesting were those tenets that run contrary to what many other investors tend to think.

For example, one of Olstein's tenets is that it is better to rely on your study of financial statements and inferences than it is to rely on discussions with management. Olstein writes, "Talking to management is an overrated function of the investment process."[23]

I agree, especially in this day and age of heightened regulatory scrutiny and litigation. Management, I've found, won't tell you much of anything you can't find or read about in publicly filed documents, press releases, and other publicly available material. You're better off talking with other smart investors.

Another tenet has to do with the quality of a company. Olstein believes quality is associated with financial strength—not with size or the number of years a company has been in business.

This, too, is contrary to the mainstream idea that large caps, the so-called blue chips, represent quality companies. I think you can find high-quality companies in obscure markets and smaller companies.

BILL MILLER—EXPLOITING TIME ARBITRAGE

Years ago, Dean LeBaron, contrarian par excellence and founder of Batterymarch Financial Management, wrote a short investment piece called "Thoughts While Not Shaving," which he supposedly wrote one summer while he was in the Swiss mountains contemplating life and not shaving.

In that spirit, I offer the following "Thoughts While Not Golfing." This was written one day when the Washington area was beset with rolling rain and thunderstorms and I was unable to play golf (though I did manage to hit a bucket of balls at the local range). Anyway, I was thinking a lot about investing.

Specifically, I was thinking a lot about "time arbitrage," an idea I'd been running across more frequently. It's a fancy and smart-sounding phrase that simply describes a strategy in which you exploit the fact that most investors (professionals and laypeople alike) have extremely short time horizons. These time horizons are usually inside of one year, meaning that you can build an advantage around simply thinking longer-term.

Proof of this short time horizon is provided in Panzner's *The New Laws of the Stock Market Jungle,* in which he shows, as mentioned earlier, that the average holding period for an NYSE stock has fallen to a matter of months.

Thinking long-term today means thinking out only a year or more. Just that amount of time, I was thinking, could give you an exploitable edge and allow you to earn superior returns. Louis Lowenstein covered this idea in his paper on successful value investors. Ralph Wanger talked about it in his interview with me.

Bill Miller, the famed manager of the Legg Mason Value Trust (which has beaten the S&P 500 for 14 years running), also talked about it in a recent interview with Value Investor Insight. Miller said, "In an environment with massive short-term data overload and with people concerned about minute-to-minute performance, the ineffi-ciencies are likely to be out beyond, say, 12 months."[24]

That's amazing. Miller says looking 12 months out can find inef-ficiencies. The investor's short-term orientation has been one of the most profound changes in markets over the last 20 years. With the Internet and the ease with which anyone can tap out trades with a few keystrokes, plus the proliferation of shortcut speculative vehicles like Exchange Traded Funds (ETFs) (basically mutual funds made up of several companies in the same industry, which then trade just like a stock)—well, add all that together and you have a very short term–oriented environment.

Exploiting that is the concept behind "time arbitrage," a term I am growing to like. It's nothing new or highly original; lots of great inves-tors have been preaching the virtues of long-term investing for years now. But in this market I believe the idea has heightened importance and immediacy.

The second thing I was rolling around in my head as I smacked my drives 300 yards (well, not 300 yards, but they always seem to go far-ther at the driving range) was the importance of thinking differently to succeed as an investor.

Miller brought this point home for me in the *Value Investor Insight* interview: "In markets, everyone tends to see the same things, read the same newspapers and get the same data feeds. The only way to arrive at a different answer from everybody else is to organize the data in dif-ferent ways and to bring things to the analytic process that are not typ-ically there."[25]

I think there is a lot in what Miller is saying. The basic idea is that if you are looking at the same stuff everybody else is, then the only way you are going to find great ideas before the herd does is to adopt a pattern of thought that is not shared by the herd.

This is one of the reasons I shy away from simple value tools such as just looking at price-earnings ratios, growth rates, or such tired concepts as businesses with great management—because everybody and their brother is already looking for those things. Thinking differently can uncover opportunities before they become apparent to the herd. When they are apparent, it is too late.

Does this sound clichéd or trite? Maybe so, but it is so important, and as much as I read about investing, I see analysts and writers routinely fall into this trap all the time. They talk about all the great things that everybody already knows and believes.

As an aside, I find Bill Miller a fascinating guy who thinks very differently from just about everybody else. He recommended a book called *Nature: An Economic History* by Geerat Vermeij. Sounds like highbrow stuff. Vermeij is a paleoecologist. That's right, paleoecologist. I didn't know such a thing existed. What he's done is take the history of evolution and apply it to economics, with interesting results. Vermeij draws insights from the natural world about how things relate, how they compete for resources, how they change and adapt, and much more.

Miller talks about how Vermeij's study provided him with a unique insight into the notion of efficiency. What Vermeij found is that efficiency is not what's important in nature. Something called "aggregation of power" is more important. In nature as well as in economics, Vermeij found, small and efficient is often crushed by bigger but less efficient.

So Miller finds that many analysts fret too much over profit margins, which, he argues, are less important than actual profits. Greater profits with lower margins may be more valuable because this creates size, and inherent in size may be certain advantages you couldn't get otherwise.

That's an uncommon insight, and it might prove useful in thinking about businesses and about the importance of profit margins versus marginal profits.

Here's another uncommon insight. This one Miller draws from another highbrow book, *Increasing Returns and Path Dependence in the Economy* by W. Brian Arthur. The basic idea is that market shares in the technology world are remarkably stable for mature applications. Therefore, Miller believes, even though technological industries are characterized by new products and short product cycles, the mature and larger companies often maintain their slices of the overall pie. Using this insight, Miller finds that Wall Street has a tendency to overestimate competitive threats.

ROY NEUBERGER'S TEN PRINCIPLES OF SUCCESSFUL INVESTING

Roy Neuberger led a remarkable life. As the co-founder of Neuberger & Berman, the multibillion-dollar investment manage-ment company, he had a long investing career. At the age of 94, he sat down and wrote his memoir—*So Far, So Good: The First 94 Years,* pub-lished in 1997. Over his 68 years on the Street, covering the meat of the tumultuous twentieth century, he never had a losing year. The man knew something about investing.

In his memoir, he offers his ten principles of successful investing:

1. *Know thyself.* The first of Neuberger's rules deals with under-standing your own strengths, weaknesses, and preferences. Are you a speculator, comfortable with taking some risks? Or are you a more conservative investor, willing to wait it out? As the old saying goes, if you don't know who you are, the market is an expensive place to find out.

2. *Study the great investors.* Neuberger lists, among them, Warren Buffett, Ben Graham, Peter Lynch, George Soros, and Jimmy Rogers. In my own newsletter, I regularly feature successful investors and entrepreneurs of the past. Many of them are not so well known—Cyrus Holliday, C. V. Starr, and Augustus Heinze among them. There are great stories here worthy of study. You can learn a great deal studying the unsuccessful investors as well. How great fortunes are lost can be even more informative than how they are won.

3. *Beware of the sheep market.* "The sheep market is a little like the fashion industry," Neuberger writes. "When a great couturier makes a new style of dress or suit, the minor designers copy it. If the hemlines on a dress go up or down, millions of people follow the fashion. That is a sheep market."[26]

    The herd instinct is strong with investors. Hearing the opin-ions of prominent analysts or media types, investors may find it hard to find their own path. The sheep market is basically one driven by crowd psychology, and it can be dangerous to your wealth to follow that market. Keep your own counsel.

4. *Keep a long-term perspective.* What is one way to immunize yourself against the suggestions of the crowd? "Keeping a long-term perspective will keep you from being diverted by fads," Neuberger writes. "There have always been fads on Wall Street, from the Stutz Bearcat autos of the 1920s to the bowling stocks of the late 1950s."[27]

Most investors spend far too much time worrying about next quarter's earnings and fretting about day-to-day, or even minute-to-minute, stock prices. Neuberger advises keeping the longer-term trends in mind and also studying the past. "Be your own historian," Neuberger writes. This bit of advice is particularly warming to me because, again, in my own newsletter I often write about the past—everything from early twentieth-century panics to the Swedish Match King and the founding of the House of Morgan. It helps to keep perspective.

All of these things make one realize that our collective financial experiences have covered just about everything. I remember reading somewhere that the only new thing in finance is the history you haven't read. I think there is a great deal of truth in that.

5. *Get in and out in time.* "Timing may not be everything, but it is a lot." Neuberger is not recommending that you become a market timer, but he emphasizes the notion that no investment is good all the time. "Everything changes," he notes. "I just don't believe you can have confidence in any industry for an infinite length of time." He also writes that it is important to recognize and close out your mistakes.[28]

6. *Analyze the companies closely.* Neuberger has a preference for tangible assets. "Check the company's real assets," Neuberger advises. Plant and equipment, real estate, natural resources, and other assets get a big plus in Neuberger's investing schema. These assets should be connected with the company's business and its ability to generate cash flow. Again, I find myself aligned with Neuberger's thinking: I like to recommend companies with piles of cash-generating assets—industrial properties, mines, hotels, airports, and more.

7. *Don't fall in love.* "One should fall in love with ideas, with people, or with idealism based on the possibilities that exist in

this adventuresome world. The last thing to fall in love with is a particular security."[29] Enough said.

8. *Diversify, but don't hedge alone.* It was Neuberger's diversification and hedging strategies that allowed him to weather the collapse of '29. He was short Radio Corporation of America, which was cut in half in the collapse and covered losses in other positions. The basic advice here is to be flexible and maintain some balance so you can pull through the unexpected dips and swirls of the market.

9. *Watch the environment.* Neuberger maintains that investors should keep an eye on general market conditions. As he says, the joys of living and investing are enhanced by an appreciation for the shifting financial seasons.

10. *Don't follow the rules.* "At least not slavishly," Neuberger adds to this last principle. Be willing to change your thinking and to challenge the thinking of others. Succeed in your own way, Neuberger advises. And remember that we all make mistakes. "Always-right investors don't exist," Neuberger concludes, "except among liars."[30]

JOHN NEFF'S DUSTY RAG AND BONE SHOP

"The investment process must begin somewhere," John Neff writes in his 1999 memoir, *John Neff on Investing.* "In my case, all ladders start in the dusty rag and bone shop of the mart, where the supply of cheap stocks replenishes itself daily."[31]

John Neff ran Vanguard's storied Windsor Fund for more than 30 years, from 1964 through 1995, where he laid down an impressive whipping of the market averages. Every $1,000 invested in his fund in 1964 had turned into $57,000 by year-end 1995, beating the return on the S&P 500 by a margin of more than two-to-one.

For that performance, Neff earned himself a place in the investors' pantheon. While Neff was not known for small-cap investing specifically, his wisdom and savvy are applicable to investors of all stripes.

Neff is often characterized, perhaps too simply, as a low price-earnings investor. It is true that he sought out stocks with low price-earnings ratios. His portfolio did not harbor the technology darlings and high-tech growth stocks of his day. More often you would find banks, home builders, autos, and airlines in Neff's portfolio. Needless to say, such self-imposed limitations did not hurt his investment performance.

But there was more to Neff's performance than simply picking out stocks with low price-earnings ratios.

Neff began his search for investment ideas by scanning the list of stocks making new lows—a list available in the *Wall Street Journal,* which often provides fresh names on a daily basis. In addition to this list, Neff liked to scan the worst performers from the previous day's action. These would be stocks that had typically fallen by 8 to 30 percent or more—the "dusty rag and bone shop" that Neff talks about.

Then Neff used what he calls the "hmmmph" test. Every once in a while, Neff would run into a familiar name on one of these lists. Some of these names would surprise him, and discovering them would elicit an audible "hmmmph." These findings would spur Neff to investigate further.

Not all of these stocks would make the cut, of course. Nonetheless, Neff showed throughout his career a remarkable ability to take advantage of temporary setbacks in the fortunes of good companies.

Admittedly, it takes some fortitude to be able to purchase these kinds of stocks. Most investors probably think they can buck the opinions of the crowd, but the evidence does not bear them out. Most investors, by definition, follow the crowd. It is extraordinarily difficult to buy a stock that just got whacked in the market.

Neff knows this and believes that it was a cornerstone of his success— his willingness to go it alone. In fact, despite his awesome track record, Neff recalls getting letters from irate shareholders and criticism in the press for some of his contrarian selections. Neff does not take his contrary philosophy too far, however. "Savvy contrarians keep their minds open, leavened by a sense of history and a sense of humor. . . . Readymade contrarian formulas supply prescriptions for failure."[32]

Windsor blazed its own path in other ways as well. While most investors—certainly the professionals—think of their portfolio in terms of industry concentration (and decide they want so much invested in oil companies, a little in tech, some in real estate, and so on), Windsor threw all that out the window.

Neff went where the values were and felt no compulsion to make sure Windsor had exposure across a wide variety of industries. If the oil sector did not offer any values for Neff, Windsor would jettison the whole sector. Most professional money managers keep some sort of asset allocation, which forces them to keep investing in sectors they do not particularly like. That's why you often hear professionals use terminology such as "underweight" and "overweight." They can't just sell a sector entirely, so they lower their exposure to it (underweight).

Windsor's freedom in this regard allowed Neff to stick his neck out. While his competitors often automatically owned the 50 largest S&P 500 companies, Windsor would often own only a couple and sometimes none at all.

This sort of approach spared Windsor shareholders the horrific losses brought on by the collapse of the Nifty Fifty stocks in the 1970s. The Nifty Fifty were a collection of blue-chip growth stocks—like Xerox, IBM, and Polaroid—that seemingly everyone owned. Needless to say, these popular stocks came crashing down.

This kind of thing happens often in markets. Lessons from such catastrophes are useful only if investors remember them, which they often don't. I'll end with a short story Neff tells to make his point.

Two hunters hire a plane to take them to a remote wilderness to go moose hunting. When they reach their destination, the pilot tells them they can each take back only one moose, because any more weight than that will strain the engine and they won't make it back.

Two days later the plane returns to pick up the hunters, and both hunters have killed two moose each. Too much weight, the pilot says. "Aww, you told us that last year, and we each gave you a $1,000 extra and you flew us back," says one of the hunters. So the pilot agrees.

Sure enough, after a short while the plane's engine sputters, and the pilot is forced to make a crash landing. Once on the ground, the dazed but unhurt hunters stagger out. "Where are we?" asks one hunter. "I don't know," replies the other, "but it sure looks a lot like where we crashed last year."

DERBY WINNERS

Because a 50–1 long shot named Giacomo won the 2005 Kentucky Derby, a few lucky trifecta punters cashed in on a $133,184 payday. Meanwhile, the hordes of bettors who plunked down money on the favorites walked away with nothing but regrets.

Betting on favorites rarely produces satisfactory results, whether at Churchill Downs or on Wall Street.

Out on the racetrack, the old-time handicappers know it's best to "copper the public," or to bet against the favorites. In the stock market, a few savvy investors have produced brilliant results by doing exactly the same thing: betting against the favorites while betting on the underdogs.

In August 2000, *Fortune* magazine published a list of its favorite stocks entitled "10 Stocks to Last the Decade." Here's a list of those companies:

Broadcom
Charles Schwab
Enron
Genentech
Morgan Stanley
Nokia
Nortel Networks
Oracle
Univision
Viacom

Pity the investors who heeded *Fortune*'s advice.

"[These stocks] were the glory stocks of the fin-de-siecle bubble," recalls Louis Lowenstein, professor of law and economic studies at Columbia University, "and their high price-earnings ratios—only one under 50—reflected the faddishness of the age. *Fortune,* swallowing the popular perceptions whole, said they were ten stocks to let you 'retire when ready.' "[33]

On the contrary, owning these stocks probably pushed retirement back several years for many of *Fortune*'s readers. Collectively, these stocks lost more than 80 percent of their value within two years. Even as the decade approaches the halfway mark, *Fortune*'s "Top 10" are still producing abysmal results.

But there were some investors who didn't own any of these names. In fact, Lowenstein, in his paper (titled "Searching for Rational Investors in a Perfect Storm"), found 10 of them. Lowenstein asked Bob Goldfarb of the well-respected value shop Sequoia Fund to select 10 funds that practice "true blue" value investment disciplines, as opposed to the many who simply wear the label. Goldfarb identified the following 10 funds for Lowenstein:

> Clipper Fund
> FPA Capital
> First Eagle Global
> Longleaf Partners
> Legg Mason Value Trust
> Mutual Beacon
> Oak Value
> Oakmark Select
> Source Capital
> Tweedy Browne American Value

(You'll notice some of these names are on the 15 best funds list in an earlier chapter.)

Lowenstein found that all of them steered clear of the names on *Fortune*'s ignominious list, with one small exception. The celebrated Bill Miller of Legg Mason owned Nokia, but since it represented less than 2 percent of his portfolio, and since he had bought it in 1996 and was holding a 1,900 percent gain—well, it's hard to be overly critical. (Mutual Beacon was actually short Viacom and Nortel.)

Lowenstein tested this group of funds for the years 1999 to 2003, which he felt were among the most volatile in recent history. During these five years the S&P 500 actually showed negative average annual returns of 0.57 percent. That's right—over the five-year stretch the market lost money. Thus, this period made a fine test for this stable of value funds.

Well, they performed brilliantly. The boring old value disciples beat the market handily over that span—earning an average annual return of 10 percent. "A five-sigma event," Lowenstein calls the achievement. "A statistical marvel that pure chance cannot explain."[34] More interesting is how they did it.

1. *Own a limited number of stocks.* Contrary to the popular wisdom that lots of stocks should be held for purposes of diversification, these investors pursued the opposite tactic. Most were fairly concentrated;

Longleaf's top five stocks often represented one-third of the value of its total portfolio.

These funds were choosy about what they put in their portfolios, and when they didn't find what they were looking for, cash filled the void. Sitting on cash is always better than doing something dumb. It's like the horseplayers who know not to bet every race. Most of these funds held large cash positions of 30 to 40 percent during the bubble years. Several were closed to new investors because they didn't want to accept any new money for which they had no compelling ideas.

The average domestic mutual fund holds about 160 stocks, compared to 54, on average, for Lowenstein's value group. In fact, 7 of the 10 value funds surveyed owned 34 stocks or less, with the average being pulled higher by the internationally diverse First Eagle and Mutual Beacon funds.

2. *Maintain a low portfolio turnover.* The average mutual fund has a turnover ratio of about 121 percent, meaning that the average fund "flips" its whole portfolio once every ten months, thus incurring heavy transaction costs while also reducing the amount of capital gains generated.

By contrast, the ten value funds held their positions for five years— on average. However, these managers don't buy and hold forever; they sell when things get pricey. Miller, for example, sold Nokia almost at the same time *Fortune* was advising readers to buy it.

3. *Look at stocks as part interests in a business.* The last trait is harder to quantify because it is not statistical in nature. Lowenstein found that these outperforming funds shared a common philosophical approach to investing—an approach inspired by Graham and Dodd, the "fathers" of value investing. "The group of ten all stands on the common ground of patient, company by company analysis," writes Lowenstein. They are "always mindful that the stocks they are buying are part interests in a business."[35] For this select group of mutual fund managers, stocks are much more than mere ticker symbols. Each represents an operating enterprise, with its own unique attributes.

Each of the funds that Lowenstein examined applies its investment philosophy in different ways. Some focus on small caps, some on large caps, and some on international stocks. But they all seem to embrace the idea that successful investing relies upon a long-term commitment to a few, well-chosen stocks.

The three main tactics common to the 10 managers Lowenstein studied all seem pretty straightforward and intuitive. Yet very few investors bother to pursue a similar approach. Bill Ruane at Sequoia Fund once estimated that only 5 percent of all professionally managed money follows the basic principles of value investing.

Instead, most investors—professional and nonprofessional alike—prefer to bet on the favorites, and that's a strategy that almost always raises the odds against you.

MORE GOOD HABITS OF INVESTING

Value Investing *Trés Chic!*

I was in Los Angeles in 2006 for a unique kind of conference. It was a gathering of the cheapskates of the investment world. These are the guys who don't like to pay much for anything, who are usually bearish on most things, and who like digging around in the trash bins and sewers of finance, trolling for overlooked goodies. It's called the Value Investing Congress. Basically, a variety of top-performing investors offered up insights and ideas over two days to a packed audience.

There was a time when holding a value investing conference would attract no more than a handful of attendees. Not today. Perhaps value investing has become popular because so many people were burned in the collapse of the tech bubble in 2000, or because flat markets over the past few years have driven people back to the basics—the kernels of investing wisdom that work and have been around for decades.

Whatever the reason, value investing now seems almost chic. And its best practitioners are rock stars. So what are today's value gurus seeing? I'll tell you about a couple of my favorite presentations.

These Industries Have Cost Investors Money—for More Than 20 Years Running

One of these presenters was J. Carlo Cannell. His lead fund, Tonga Partners, has earned 25 percent annually since 1992. That's a great track record.

Cannell, an easygoing, West Coast kind of guy, stood up there in his khakis and casual shirt and talked about short selling—a way to make money when stocks go down.

I don't recommend short selling in my newsletter, but Cannell's presentation had some fascinating information—useful stuff even for us longs. Here's the deal: Most people think short selling is not a smart thing to do. Cannell knows this.

He started his presentation by showing how various market indexes have gone up a whole lot over time. And he used a short index devised by CSFB/Tremont that shows how shorts have lost money since 1994 (the earliest data available for this index).

Basically, he was recognizing one of the key arguments against short selling: Don't fight the tape. Or don't try to swim upstream. You get the picture.

But here is where it gets interesting. Cannell then chose several industries that have not made money for investors, on average, for years. These are the opportunities you want to short—if you're a short seller. If you are an investor, you should tread very carefully here.

Airlines have been horrible investments. Since 1983, investors have basically lost money. There are 14 companies in Cannell's index, and the compound annual growth rate (CAGR) is about minus 6.5 percent annually.

By the way, these numbers make things look better than they actually were for most investors. These losses are only the losses experienced by surviving investors—incredibly, these numbers don't include the big zeroes. Doing so would have led to even lower returns.

Let's take a look at computer hardware manufacturers, another graveyard of investment returns.

There are 68 names in this index. Again, the results are horrible, with negative 13 percent annual returns. Computer hardware has been a tough business for investors.

Look at semiconductor equipment manufacturers and restaurants. Again, these industries have cost investors money for over 20 years running. A 4 percent annual loss for semiconductor equipment companies and another 4 percent annual loss for restaurants.

The key takeaway here is that these businesses represent areas that have been very tough places to make money not only for a long stretch of time—since 1983—but for a period that has covered one of the best bull markets in stocks in history. If a business can't generate a positive return for investors over that stretch, when will it? So again, investors ought to have strong reasons for holding stocks in these industries, which, for the most part, have been investor graveyards.

Mohnish Pabrai—The Dhandho Investor

My favorite speaker was Mohnish Pabrai, and not because I was so interested in his stock pick. (It was Berkshire Hathaway, which, by the way, was probably the most talked-about stock at the conference. Everybody seemed to think it was a bargain.) I liked Pabrai because he had interesting insights into investing. And he told a pretty cool story about Mr. B. U. Patel.

B. U. Patel is the founder and CEO of Tarsadia Hotels and probably the richest South Asian in southern California. He started with one 20-room motel in Anaheim and eventually grew this to over 4,400 rooms across America—becoming one of the dominant motel operators.

Apparently, the Patels were refugees from East Africa. They had a strong entrepreneurial drive and a smart sense about value. They strived to put themselves in situations in which they could make a lot or lose a little. Such situations made them say, "Dhandho!" Literally translated, it means, "Business!" But the connotation was "a very good deal." Or as Pabrai put it, "Heads I win, tails I don't lose much."

Anyway, the Patels would buy a motel for little money down, move their clan in, and fire all the workers. The family then ran the motel and dropped prices. In a short amount of time, they would fill up the motel and earn lots of cash. Then they would take their money and do it again . . . and again and again. Each time they reinvested in new motels in similar situations.

In time they became the dominant motel operator in the country. About a third of all U.S. motels are operated by the Patels—that's about a $40 billion enterprise. Pabrai's point in telling this story was to show how they only looked for situations in which they could make a lot and lose a little.

Pabrai created a list of what he called the "Dhandho Framework," which outlines the Patel philosophy. It is a nice little model for investors:

1. Invest in simple, unchanging businesses.
2. Focus on distressed businesses/industries.
3. Invest in businesses with durable moats.
4. Make few bets, big bets, or infrequent bets.
5. Fixate on arbitrage.
6. Watch the margin of safety—always!
7. Heads I win, tails I don't lose much!
8. Copycats trump the innovators.

Most of these are self-evident. A couple of them could use a little explaining. Number 5 simply means that the Patels are looking to take advantage of relatively easy opportunities. For instance, it was a simple matter whenever they acquired a new motel to fire all the existing workers—which represented huge cost savings—and replace them with family members.

Eventually this gap closed as the Patels themselves got bigger and began to run into competition that copied their methods. Investors, too, look to fill gaps that will close over time—but in that time they can make a lot of money.

Number 8 is interesting, too. Pabrai quoted the work of Amar Bhide, who found that most Inc. 500 entrepreneurs had lifted their business idea from a former employer—and many times the employer was not even interested in the idea.

Microsoft is an example of a copycat company as opposed to an innovator. It is chock-full of technologies that it bought, copied, or lifted from competitors and other companies.

This is why Pabrai believes that in the battle between Microsoft and Google it will be no contest. Microsoft will win, hands down because, according to Pabrai, this kind of copycat competitiveness is embedded in the company DNA. Google, on the other hand, is an innovator and makes most of its own stuff. Microsoft knows how to fight dirty in the trenches and get what it needs by whatever means necessary. In the long run, history shows, the trench fighter will win more often than not.

Pabrai has a solid track record as well, beating all the major indexes and 99 percent of all funds since the inception of his fund. He runs a tight portfolio of only about a dozen names. He makes big bets, holds on to his stocks, and "takes naps in the afternoon." You gotta love that. For those interested, I highly recommend his book *Mosaic: Perspectives on Investing* and also his latest book, *Dhandho Investor*.

ANTHONY BOLTON—THE PETER LYNCH OF BRITAIN

Here's an investor you've probably never heard of. Yet he's enjoyed a 20 percent compound annual return for more than a quarter of a century managing one of the largest mutual funds in the United Kingdom. Such a sustained record of excellence has earned him a number of superlatives, as well as the sobriquet "the Peter Lynch of Britain."

I'm a sucker for books exploring the careers and experiences of great investors. I read far and wide in this field. Basically, I look at it as a way to keep learning and improving my own methods.

Moreover, I have come to believe that there are core elements to successful long-term investing that run through all of these stories of great investors. It never hurts to revisit these core principles. Nor do I ever tire of learning from the experiences of investors who have been in the game a long time.

It was with these thoughts in mind that I recently picked up a book by Jonathan Davis titled *Investing with Anthony Bolton: The Anatomy of a Stock Market Phenomenon*. The book, published in England by Harriman House, got practically no coverage in the United States when it came out in 2004. I only found out about it by reading the *Financial Times,* in which a writer mentioned it in passing.

Anthony Bolton is the investor behind that sterling track record. He runs the Fidelity Special Situations Fund (U.K.). In this slim volume, I found some simple—but enduring—insights that I would like to pass on to you.

Bolton works in the heart of London in an office block overlooking St. Paul's Cathedral. His guiding philosophy is the beginning of investment wisdom. You can't be afraid to stray from the herd, and you ought to relish turning over stones that the rest of the market may be missing. Also, don't do a lot of "dealing" (trading), as he says. Give your ideas time to work out. Think long–term, meaning years, not months. In these investment principles, Bolton is not very different from many of the greatest American investors.

There are other common threads, though. I'm always interested in the failures. Disasters seem an unavoidable part of the investor's experience. Play the game long enough and you are bound to make a serious mistake. Bolton has had his share of disasters, investing in companies that ultimately went bust.

Then there are those times when the portfolio as a whole turns in a lackluster performance. In 1990 Bolton's fund lost 28.8 percent of its value for the year. He followed that with a paltry 3 percent return in 1991. That's a two-year stretch when investors didn't make any money following one of the greatest investors of our time. However, despite this period—and others—in which Bolton trailed the market or lost money, his overall track record puts him in the investing hall of fame.

Bolton writes:

> Investment is an odds game. No one gets it right all the time; we are all trying to make fewer mistakes than our competitors. In fact, the key to this business is as much to avoid losers as it is to pick winners. On the other hand, running money with a style that is so defensive that it avoids all losers is also, I believe, counterproductive to superior returns.[36]

Bolton has the ability to "shrug off the occasional failure . . . confident that the gains will on average outnumber the duds."[37] Investing takes some measure of courage. You can't believe every flesh wound is mortal. Part of successful investing is an ability to stick to your discipline, even during stretches when it appears not to be working well. Bolton, like many great investors, does not switch horses midrace.

That doesn't mean he is sure of everything he is doing. And this is an interesting psychological part of investing that you don't hear all that much about. "Conviction waxes and wanes," Bolton writes, "and a lot of the time, you're uncertain about everything."[38] When conviction is high, then you make big bets. When conviction is low, you should sit on the sidelines or invest smaller amounts.

One misconception people have about the great investors is that they are always sure of what they are doing. "Some seem to think people like myself are hugely sure of what they are doing all the time," he says. "But this business is not like that. You are in a constant state of questioning your convictions."[39]

Bolton also does not spend much time on macro forecasting. He does not base his investment decisions on broad macroeconomic grounds alone. He instead works to understand individual companies. This is where you can build an edge. He invokes fellow Briton Jim Slater's Zulu Principle—"If you are expert on something, however small it may be in the broader context of things, you have an advantage over other people."[40]

Bolton also focuses on balance sheets, as I do. The balance sheet is a summary of a company's assets and liabilities, a snapshot of financial strength. "One vital lesson I have learned," Bolton writes, "is that when things go wrong, the companies I lost the most money on are those with weak balance sheets."[41] Most analysts and investors are not good at understanding balance sheets and assessing these risks. I've got 10 years of lending experience, which taught me a lot about risk and the meaning of financial strength. Most investors have little real-world business experience.

In addition to balance sheets, Bolton focuses on cash flow. Again, this has always been a hallmark of *Capital & Crisis*. I focus on cash-generating activities, not necessarily on pretty earnings pictures drawn up for the benefit of Wall Street. "The ability to generate cash is a very attractive attribute," Bolton says. "In fact, the most favorable of all attributes."[42]

Finally, it was refreshing to hear Bolton try to explain his investment style. What is it? What do you do? As an investment writer, I, too, often get this question, and it is never easy to answer in a sound-bite sort of way. As Bolton answered, "Trying to explain what makes me buy one stock and not another is surprisingly difficult, even after all these years."[43] Further confirmation that the best investing philosophies cannot be packaged neatly in boxes for public consumption.

Investing is a qualitative art or skill honed over many years. In a similar way, a painter or woodcarver might master certain techniques over a lifetime, yet not be able to teach them easily to a newcomer. It is not easy to teach these ideas, and they are not always easily articulated.

I hope this brief look at Bolton's thinking has given you some basics of his style. I've shared with you some of his more timeless and universal aspects. Bolton will be stepping down at the end of 2007, at the age of 56. His long, successful run at Fidelity, though, ensures him a place in investing Valhalla.

BRUCE BERKOWITZ—BET THE JOCKEY, NOT THE HORSE

Adam Smith (the pen name of author George Goodman, not the eighteenth-century economist) tells the story of meeting Ben Graham one day in New York in 1970.

Graham, at the time, was 76 years old. He lived in the South of France, with his lady friend, translating Greek and Latin classics. He had long since retired from the rough-and-tumble world of markets and Wall Street.

Graham liked Smith's book and liked his style. He wrote Smith a letter telling him that he had something to discuss with Smith when he came to New York.

And so it was that in 1970 Adam Smith met Benjamin Graham for the first time. The grand old man had a request for the talented Mr. Smith. Graham told Smith that he wanted him to work on the next edition of *The Intelligent Investor,* which was Graham's celebrated book on investing (still in print today).

"There are only two people I would ask to do this," Graham said. "You are one, and Warren Buffett is the other."

"Who is Warren Buffett?" Smith asked.[44]

The thing is, even in 1970 Buffett had a superb track record. He started his partnership with $105,000 cobbled together from friends and relatives. When he closed that partnership in 1969, it had $105 million—and it had generated a compound annual return of 31 percent per year. Buffett himself was worth $25 million, a handsome sum even today.

Every great investor was once an unknown. That is not saying much. But even after they put in dazzling performances, it's amazing to me how many terrific investors stay on the fringe of the public's consciousness. Others with far less skill manage far more money. Others with inferior track records enjoy the enriching rays of the spotlight.

It seems hard to imagine in this day and age that any superb talent could escape notice, as Warren Buffett seemed to do in 1970. Especially given the efficiency of the Internet as the world's greatest grapevine.

Yet I think it still happens that great investors slip under the public's radar.

The Fairholme Fund is not familiar to most investors, I would guess. Bruce Berkowitz, the founder and top dog, is the kind of guy no one would recognize in a lineup as a top-performing investor. Yet, since its inception in 1999, investors in his fund have enjoyed a 19 percent annual return compared to a negative 1 percent return for the S&P 500 over that time.

That is truly an outstanding performance. And while the Fairholme Fund enjoys a five-star fund rating from Morningstar, it is not really a big fund: It has about $3 billion in assets and is in the top quartile of Morningstar's universe, but that's a top-heavy universe. There are hundreds of funds with $50 billion, $60 billion, $70 billion, or more. There are several with over $100 billion under management. And Fairholme is just one fund with no sisters. Many funds belong to a family with lots of other funds—like Fidelity or Vanguard.

I should note that Fairholme did this while holding a lot of cash. Normally it is only 75 percent invested. That makes its performance all the more impressive.

Fairholme ably explains its playbook on its web page. It is a familiar system. "We stay away from faddish companies, industries, or trends and routinely shun companies that employ aggressive accounting or managers that are paid fortunes just to show up to work every day." They concentrate their portfolio in their best 15 to 20 ideas, "backed by intrinsic value that has been glossed over, misunderstood or unappreciated by the marketplace."[45]

If you go to Fairholme's web site (http://www.fairholmefunds .com), you'll see a section called "Fairholme's Maxims: A Primer to Value Investing," which I would encourage you to read.

Berkowitz may never achieve quite the fame or track record of Warren Buffett. But I'm betting that shareholders in his fund don't mind. He's doing quite all right for them.

CHARLES KOCH—HIS 100-BAGGER

Charles Koch is the 70-year-old skipper (as I write) behind Koch Industries. The company is the largest privately held company in the world, recently passing Cargill with its purchase of Georgia-Pacific.

Koch is an interesting story on a couple of levels. On the surface, it's a great success story. Charles Koch may not be the greatest investor who "ever hoofed the verdure of God's green footstool" (to borrow from the inimitable H. L. Mencken), but he ought to be somewhere up there in the rarefied air of investing Valhalla.

That's because the value of Koch Industries has increased 100-fold in the 38 years he has been running the show, compared with a 13-fold increase in the S&P 500 over that time span.

If Koch were just another success story, he wouldn't have interested me as much. What makes his story so compelling is the manner in which his fortune grew.

For instance, there were some tremendous failures along the way. Koch lost $50 million betting on supertankers and crude oil in the 1970s. He also lost $120 million trying to turn Purina—which would eventually go bankrupt—into an integrated agribusiness in the 1990s. The mistakes that investors make fascinate me. And I'm always struck by how even the best investors make big mistakes at times—yet still wind up with a fortune.

Koch says he gets burned a lot. If only we could all get burned like Koch. Despite these errors, Koch Industries has thrived, and Koch remains unafraid of making mistakes. Running a private company facilitates this attitude: he doesn't have to answer to Wall Street and its focus on quarterly results. It's hard to be contrarian in a fishbowl. Instead, Koch can make good decisions based on long-term thinking.

Koch Industries recently purchased Georgia-Pacific at a 39 percent premium to the stock market price. Georgia-Pacific is in an ugly business—pulp and paper. Worse, the company is saddled with 57,000 asbestos lawsuits.

"I like deals with hair on them," Koch says. "If a business doesn't have complications, it's probably too expensive for us."[46]

Koch counts Austrian economists Friedrich Hayek and Ludwig von Mises among his favorite influences. Mises had a big impact on my thinking as well, and his work gave me invaluable insights into how markets work.

Koch was fascinated by the creative destruction and ever-changing nature of markets. "You constantly have to destroy what you're doing," Koch says.[47]

All in all, Charles Koch and Koch Industries make a good story. And for investors, that story teaches us several things—the benefits of being unafraid of failure, the need to think long-term, and the importance of wandering from the herd.

DAVID BABSON—INVESTMENT FOLK HERO

There is a theory which states that if anyone discovers exactly what the Universe is for and why it is here, it will instantly disappear and be replaced by something even more bizarre and inexplicable. . . . There is another which states this has already happened.
      —*Douglas Adams,* The Restaurant at the End of the Universe

My five-year-old daughter heard the Rolling Stones song "You Can't Always Get What You Want." To which she added, "This song is a truth I already know."

Yes, we all learn pretty fast that we can't always get what we want. As investors, not every year can be 1982, when you could buy just about anything because just about everything was cheap. Every investor must make do with the market he finds himself in.

Most of the time bargains are hard to find. Like now. In times like this, I like to look back.

Investors, like practitioners of other trades, are guided by precedent. And so I spend a good bit of time poring over old books and looking over nuggets of market history, like a geologist picking up bits of rock. In those layers of sediment lie answers.

In this history, you will find ballast for those times when the rest of the market seems to go nuts. The historical record reminds us that common sense ultimately prevails. Herds, as a rule, make for poor investors.

Let's look at the stock market of the 1960s, a maddening maelstrom of a market. All in all, it was not so different from the raging tech bubble of the late 1990s.

National Student Marketing was the poster child of the era. Here was a company designed to capture the "youth market." The company bought everything and anything that might aid it in this quest. It owned youth-oriented travel agencies and insurance companies, college ring makers, college mug manufacturers, and more. At its great height, it was selling for 150 times earnings.

Yet look who owned National Student Marketing. Bankers Trust and Morgan Guaranty, as well as General Electric's pension fund. The endowments at Harvard, Cornell, and the University of Chicago.

Yes, the old money of banks, pension funds, and endowments. These are the people to whom the uninitiated turn for trusted advice. These are the people who are supposed to protect and grow their clients' wealth.

In 1970 National Student Marketing went from $36 to $1. There were many others just like it.

The modern-day Adam Smith hatched an unusual idea for an investment conference in 1970. Instead of the usual fare—speakers talking about their successes and favorite ideas—Smith thought it might be good to have something of a public confessional.

His would be a conference where people talked about their mistakes and misdeeds. Smith thought this would be good for the confessors and extremely instructive for the audience. Especially after the go-go market of the 1960s met its inevitable bad end.

David Babson, our protagonist, was one of those invited to speak at Smith's conference. Babson, then turning 60, ran the sixth-largest investment counseling business in the country at the time.

A little background on Babson sets the stage. He started his firm in 1940. He was bullish then. Babson recommended buying growth stocks, a move that made him a radical in those days when the memories of the Great Depression were still fresh. He bought what seemed to be all the right stocks—3M, Honeywell, Merck, Pfizer, Corning Glass, and others.

By the 1960s, though, Babson was no longer bullish. The feisty, pipe-smoking New Englander was blunt and outspoken in chastising his peers for behaving like tape-watching speculators. He had become a trenchant critic of the market, which was a swirling stew of gimmickry, malfeasance, and excessive speculation. Babson blasted his peers for "outright gambling with other people's money," and he called the stock market a "national craps game."

Just as Babson found himself out of step with the 1940s, so he found himself out of step again in the 1960s.

As Smith's unusual conference got under way, Smith thought it was going pretty much as intended. Then he tapped Babson for comments. Babson took the stage and addressed the crowd. Smith asked if the blame should go to the professionals for the sixties bubble. Babson said yes, unequivocally, in so many words. "What should be done about this?" Smith asked.

And that's when Babson, peering over his glasses to gaze down at the audience, delivered his knockout blow: "Some of you should leave this business," he said.

As Smith reported later, there was nervous laughter among the attendees. Then Babson practically named names and launched into an accusatory tongue-lashing in which he lambasted the folly and incompetence of his peers. Smith finally stopped him, but the conference had, as Smith noted, "taken a sour turn." The audience sat in stunned silence.

Babson could say what he did because he didn't own any of the nonsense stocks. He had also solidified his status as an investment folk hero for his courage and independence. Not to mention the gratitude of his clients, who escaped the 1960s with their money intact.

A surging market surely will provide sins for future confessionals— every market does. After all, what investment adviser could possibly justify putting his clients' hard-earned money into something as unsound as Research In Motion in late 2006. The maker of the Blackberry device was posting slowing growth rates, facing numerous competitors, and trading for more than 10 times sales and 60 times trailing earnings.

Yet these stocks find votaries among the pros. Look at who owns them. All the big houses—Fidelity, Barclays, Wellington, banks, and trusts of various types. What are their investors paying them for?

So far these stocks have kept going up. In the latter part of 2006, they rallied sharply, as did the market as whole. One day the caffeine will wear off, however, and with it the temporary illusion that these stocks are worth these prices. It seems only a matter of time.

Markets are notoriously hard to read. People see what they want to see. Bulls will find reasons why these stocks will go higher. Bears will find reasons for them to go lower. The seldom-admitted truth is that most of the time the market exists in some indeterminate state, like the muddled cherry of a whiskey sour.

I think the main lesson from Babson is that you cannot trust consensus. You cannot rely on "the establishment." You can't find refuge in the herd. And you must resist the urge to join the crowd. "Passion of the moment," as writer J. P. Donleavy observed, "[is] a disaster over the years."

Babson's firm, by the way, lives on. Recently, it published a letter describing five essential truths the firm follows, laid out by its founder years ago. They are:

1. Markets are unpredictable and ill suited to forecasts.
2. Long-term fundamentals are key.
3. Investor emotion leads to volatility.
4. Valuation discipline should guide investment selection.
5. Perspective and patience are rewarded.

That's not a bad set of self-explanatory truths. They are not sexy, but the best investment advice seldom is. Investors would do well to remember them—and remember Babson—when considering whether they should plunge in and buy the hot stocks of the day.

CHRIS BROWNE—DOUBLE YOUR CHANCES OF FINDING GREAT INVESTMENTS

Christopher Browne of Tweedy Browne fame wrote a book called *The Little Book of Value Investing*. In it, he lays out some basic thoughts and ideas on how the aspiring investor might add to his financial breadbasket.

The book is in the Graham & Dodd tradition: it espouses simple verities about the virtues of buying cheap stocks. It's like a little country store. But instead of polished apples and sweet corn, the shelves hold bags of polished wisdom and sweet dollops of moneymaking advice.

But what struck me, buried among the homespun maxims, was Browne's emphasis on global investing.

Browne gleefully tells readers of his exploits kicking around in faraway markets. Like an eager traveler returning from his first look at the pyramids of Egypt or gazing up at the Incan ruins of Machu Picchu, Browne talks about the glories of picking up cheap stocks in Japan, South Korea, and Switzerland.

In the late 1990s, free-spirited investors could find Japanese home builders, media companies, and textile mills selling for less than the cash on their books. In 2003 Browne uncovered a Swiss conglomerate loaded with valuable assets—real estate, a sheet metal business, a sporting goods division, and more. The stock traded for only one-half of an understated book value. In two years the stock doubled. He writes about Dae Han Flour Mills of South Korea, which he picked up for one-third of book value.

This is merely a small sample of Browne's profit-laden travelogue. A globetrotting treasure hunter, Browne spends considerable ink on topics such as the rationale behind global investing, understanding foreign accounting, and what to make of foreign currencies.

But for all the convoluted reasons others often offer up for investing in foreign stocks, Browne offers one that's crystal clear. "If you expand your horizons to all the developed countries of the world," he writes, "you can double your chances of finding cheap stocks."[48]

To dispel any fears of putting your hard-earned dough in some flighty company glued together with matchsticks, Browne offers another basic, yet compelling, observation.

When you rank the top 20 companies in the world by sales, you find that 12 of them maintain headquarters in Europe or Asia. "The world's largest oil company [BP] is based in the United Kingdom," Browne writes. "And three of the five largest auto manufacturers are found in Germany and Japan."[49]

What holds true at the top also holds true in the middle and the bottom. There are good midsize and small companies tucked away in places other than the United States. Stateside investors who ignore these other opportunities are like wine drinkers who don't want to try imported wines. They have restricted their choices unnecessarily—and they don't know what they are missing.

Browne is a man who follows his own recipes. Today his firm, Tweedy Browne, is finding bargains overseas. Of the $14 billion in assets it manages, about 70 percent is in international stocks. And about one-third of that is in small companies with a market cap of $5 billion or less. Among his current favorites spots are South Korea, Japan, and Mexico.

Another good reason to invest abroad is to give you some exposure to a currency other than the frail and waning dollar. In 2005 Brazil's market rose about 30 percent. However, the Brazilian real also rose against the dollar by about 14 percent. So, all told, U.S.-based investors in Brazilian stocks turned a 30 percent market gain into a 50 percent gain in dollar terms.

Not that you will always get that extra wind behind your back. But it shows you an unappreciated force in global investing.

In summary, plenty of options lie before investors these days. Consider the opening up of eastern Europe or the booming economies of Asia. Or look at the brightening prospects in parts of Africa. Or easily overlooked South America.

Chris Browne reminds us of the potential in these markets. He nudges us to take a look beyond the fringe of trees on the horizon and explore other lands under the big open sky.

MAX GUNTHER—THE ZURICH AXIOMS

> *The Swiss are among the most affluent people in the world. . . . How do the Swiss do it? They do it by being the world's cleverest investors, speculators and gamblers.*
>
> —*Max Gunther,* The Zurich Axioms

What Gunther says here may or may not be true. Readers, though, should forgive Gunther for his bias. He is Swiss, for one thing. For another, his father was a member of a club of Swiss stock and commodity investor-traders who gathered in Wall Street after World War II. They met informally at Oscar's Delmonico and other favored Wall Street watering holes. They enjoyed each other's company, shared a desire for good food and drink, and also wanted to get rich. In this, they also shared the belief that no one ever gets rich off a salary.

The Swiss surely hold no monopoly in the trade of wealth creation. But the members of this postwar club had a set of ideas they dubbed the "Zurich Axioms." There were 12 major axioms and a host of lesser ones. Gunther, a witty writer, set out to codify these precepts in his book *The Zurich Axioms,* published in 1985.

The axioms are entertaining and thought-provoking. And as Gunther writes, "They are not just a philosophy of speculation; they are guideposts for successful living. They have made a lot of people rich."[50]

I won't go through all 12. But I'll hit the one Gunther says may be the most important of all. It's the fifth axiom: "On Patterns: Chaos is not dangerous until it begins to look orderly." Put simply, this axiom emphasizes that the market is a world that does not adhere to any patterns or laws. "Arguing with it is like standing in a blizzard and howling that it wasn't supposed to arrive until tomorrow."[51] The market is no respecter of logic or rational prediction.

"Patterns seem to appear in it from time to time," Gunther writes, "as do patterns in a cloudy sky or in the froth at the edge of the ocean. But they are ephemeral. They are not a sound basis on which to base one's plans."[52] Hence, the axiom dispenses with the illusion that there is a reliable formula to get rich.

Instead, the axiom acknowledges the role of chance and luck. "Any half-baked moneymaking scheme will work when you are lucky," writes Gunther. "No scheme will work when you are unlucky." He calls this "the axiom's great, liberating truth."[53]

Knowing this, investors learn never to trust "systems" or rely on predictions about the future. Forecasts on oil, the economy, and interest rates—take it all and chuck it. Read for awareness and entertainment, but don't bet on them.

Related to this is the "historian's trap": Because event B followed event A at some similar time in the past, it will do so again. History never repeats itself reliably enough for anyone to prudently make a buck on it. In investing, we see this in the "chartist's illusion": People believe stock charts hold some insight into the future. As Gunther writes: "The hucksters and con artists of the world have been aware of the power of charts for centuries."[54] The power, that is, to sell someone else on what is supposed to be a moneymaking scheme.

Finally, this axiom comes into play on all those correlations people presume to be true in markets. They look for links in cause and effect where none exist—focusing on chart patterns or price-earnings ratios or other simple metrics and supposed historical relationships. Gunther relates an old story that has been told many different ways:

> A fellow stands on a street corner every day waving his arms and uttering strange cries. A cop goes up to him one day and asks what it's all about. "I'm keeping the giraffes away," the fellow explains. "But we've never had any giraffes around here," says the cop. "Doing a good job, ain't I?" says the fellow.[55]

ANNIE OAKLEY—THE BUTTERFLY EFFECT AND YOU

In the late 1800s, Buffalo Bill's Wild West Show was a dazzling display of horsemanship, gunplay, and other cowboy skills. One of its acts involved the sharpshooting of the great Annie Oakley. Dubbed "Little Sure Shot," Oakley had an amazing routine—she would shoot out lit candles, for example, and the corks out of wine bottles.

For her grand finale, she would shoot out the lit end of a cigarette held in a man's mouth from a certain distance. For this, she would ask for volunteers from the audience. As no one ever volunteered, she would have her husband planted among the spectators. He would "volunteer," and they would complete the dangerous trick together.

Well, during one swing through Europe, Oakley was setting up her finale, and she asked for volunteers. To her shock—and the surprise of everyone involved with the show—she got a real volunteer.

The proud young Prince (soon to be Kaiser) Wilhelm bravely stepped down from among the spectators, strode into the ring, and stuck a lit cigarette in his mouth.

Reportedly out late the night before enjoying the local beer gardens, Annie was unnerved by the unexpected appearance of this famous volunteer. But the show must go on.

She took aim and fired . . . putting out the cigarette, much to Wilhelm's amusement.

Thus, she also created one of historians' favorite "what if" moments. What if her bullet had gone through the future Kaiser's left ear? Would World War I have happened? Would the lives of 8.5 million soldiers and 13 million civilians have been spared? Would Hitler have risen from the ashes of defeated Germany? All sorts of questions come to light.

Scientists call these kinds of episodes *frozen accidents*—points in time where small changes in events would have had dramatic consequences. Eric Beinhocker relates Oakley's tale in his new book *Origin of Wealth*— which is, in part, a look at the unpredictable nature of markets.

The market itself is an accumulation of frozen accidents. Stock prices don't always move smoothly from one tick to the next. Seemingly imperceptible changes at the margin can lead to outsized changes in stock prices. The classic metaphor for this process is that of a butterfly flapping its wings in Brazil and setting off a chain of events that lead to a hurricane in Texas.

One great example of this "butterfly effect" is the crazy ride of Imperial Sugar. What small change caused this stock to more than double in a year's time? Basically, there was a bull market in oil. And few drew the conclusion that people would start burning food for fuel. But the biofuel boom has been good for agricultural products and agricultural producers, including sugar refineries, as the price of Imperial Sugar's stock illustrates.

Then there is Gold Kist, the nation's third-largest chicken producer. The stock was more than cut in half from its high. What happened? A man gets sick in Asia, setting off a chain of events that puts the entire American chicken industry into a depression as prices of chicken meat tumble—even though you can't get bird flu from eating a cooked chicken and even though there have been no reported instances of bird flu in the United States.

In this case, the value of the business held up much better than the stock price. Pilgrim's Pride realized that and made an offer to buy the company—at a 50 percent premium.

The conclusion here is this: The market, like life in general, is full of surprises. No one can predict its movements consistently. The market is too dynamic, too complex. Beinhocker advises investors to keep an adaptive and highly pragmatic mind-set that "values tangible facts about today more than guesses about tomorrow."[56]

As investors, you can make that uncertainty work for you. Focus on what you are getting for your money today. Look to back that purchase price with loads of tangible assets and/or a super-strong financial condition. Then your portfolio will be better equipped to handle those instances when a sure shot misses its mark.

MARK TIER—TIMELESS WEALTH-BUILDING SECRETS

There are really no "secrets" about how to invest successfully. There are lots of good ideas out there in plain sight—in books, newsletters, magazines, and more—and you can acquire them cheaply. The problem is that there are lots of really bad ideas about investing out there, too. Most people can't tell the difference between the two. This makes it hard to create a winning investment strategy. It's like trying to make peach pie without knowing a ripe peach from a rotten one. That's problem number one.

The second difficulty is that even when you find the genuine article—a timeless bit of investing wisdom—it is not something you can use to great effect in isolation. In other words, the "secret" to creating a successful investing strategy is about combining some great ideas with other great ideas. Knowing one idea is like having a 16-step recipe and knowing only step number 6. You need to know all that comes before and after step 6 to make the recipe work well.

Finally, there are a lot of great recipes. Meaning, there are many great investors who have made fortunes in a number of different ways. Some of these recipes are relatively simple, and some are rather intricate. The variety just makes it harder for the aspiring master investor to figure out what the heck to do.

Given all this, creating a profitable investment philosophy appears daunting. And yet, there are some winning habits that characterize nearly all the great investors. Plus, there are some basic observations that should be useful to anyone trying to figure out which recipe to follow or to those trying to make their own recipes.

Mark Tier, in his book *The Winning Investment Habits of Warren Buffet & George Soros,* begins with a sound premise, one that I use myself in studying investing: study the greatest investors. This immediately limits the field. It eliminates the talking heads on television and radio and wipes out the authors of most books and magazine articles.

The greatest investors have long track records, measured in decades. (And don't limit yourself to the living—I've learned many things from studying the dead investors of long ago.) The subtitle of his book is "Harness the Investment Genius of the World's Richest Investors." This gives you some idea of his method.

The book is mainly about Buffett and Soros, two great investors who probably need no introduction. Tier's book walks you through 23 winning investment habits (as well as 7 deadly investment sins) that he maintains are shared by all the great investors he's studied. Let's go through some of those habits. Perhaps you can add these to your repertoire and start seeing immediate results.

Bet big. In the hands of some novice investors, this advice is financial suicide. But the fact remains that many of the great investors got that way by making big bets on their favorite ideas instead of spreading out their money over many smaller positions.

Tier relates a great story in his book about George Soros. A trader has put on a successful trade, and Soros asks him about the size of his position. "One billion dollars," the trader confidently reports. Soros's next comment has since become part of Wall Street lore. Soros said: "You call that a position?" He encouraged the trader to double his position.[57]

Making big bets goes counter to mainstream financial advice, which encourages balanced portfolios that have a little bit in stocks and bonds, are diversified across sectors, and so on. Yet such diversification only prevents you from losing a lot of money. No one ever got rich following a great diversification strategy.

Of course, betting big without having a well-thought-out investment strategy is probably a recipe for disaster. You need more than just this single idea—which gets back to what I was saying about great ideas working in combination. Anyway, let's go through a few more.

Start with the As. One of my favorite Buffett anecdotes in the book goes like this: A reporter asks Buffett where he gets his investment ideas. He replies that he reads annual reports and learns about every company in the United States with publicly traded securities. "But there are twenty-seven thousand public companies," the reporter responds. "Well," replies Buffett, "start with the As."[58]

What's great about this story is how well it illustrates the diligence of great investors. They are constantly searching for new investment ideas. And the scope of their search is extensive. You have to read a lot and read widely.

When there's nothing to do—do nothing. "You don't get paid for *activity,*" Buffett once told shareholders at his annual meeting. "You only get paid for being *right.*" If there's one thing I would tell an aspiring investor, it would be this. Learn when to do nothing.

When there are no fat pitches to swing at, you have to be content to just wait it out. Don't invest just because you have the cash. Let the opportunities drive your buy decisions. As Jim Rogers (of *Investment Biker* fame and once a partner of George Soros) puts it, "One of the best rules anybody can learn about investing is to do nothing, absolutely nothing, unless there is something to do."[59]

Most investors feel like they have to be doing something. As Tier writes, "Waiting is alien to his mentality because, without criteria, he has no idea what to wait for."[60] Master investors, according to Tier, are like gold prospectors. They know exactly what they are looking for—and they keep searching until they find gold.

Know when to sell. Most investors seem to have little idea about when to sell. They sell when their stocks go up in price. They sell when they go down. There is little to guide the sell decision other than emotion and stock price changes.

Buffett sells under three conditions. First, he sells if the business is broken in some way and no longer meets his criteria. Second, he sells if he needs the money to fund an even better opportunity (something he hasn't had to do in many years, since he has been in the position of having more cash than good ideas in recent years). Third, he sells if he realizes he's made a mistake.

Tier goes through other examples of possible sell strategies, but for the long-term investor—who studies and invests by the fundamentals of a business—Buffett's rules are the best.

Master the craft. "I have enjoyed the process [of making money] far more than the proceeds," Buffett once wrote, "though I have learned to live with those also."[61] Ever wonder what could motivate a billionaire investor to keep going long after he's already made his fortune? Tier finds that the great investors are emotionally involved and get satisfaction from the process of investing.

"For many successful investors," Tier writes, "the most rewarding and exciting part of the process is the search, not the investment he eventually finds." He quotes one investor as saying, "Investing is like a giant treasure hunt. I love the hunt."[62]

So the final and great irony in all of this is that to get rich you have to love the game. When the money doesn't matter so much is when the money comes. Life works in funny ways. And investing is no different.

CHAPTER 6

WHEN TO SELL

In investing it is never wrong to change your mind. It is only wrong to change your mind and do nothing about it.

—Seth Klarman, *Margin of Safety*

The Astor family fortune was among the largest in nineteenth-century America. Its roots go back to John Jacob Astor, a butcher's son and immigrant from Walldorf, Germany. For a time Astor was no more than a peddler of fur skins and cheap jewelry. But he was full of zest, ambition, and street smarts, and before long he had an expansive network of trappers and agents in his employ.

Through his network he could obtain furs for a dollar a piece, and then he would ship them to places like London, where they could be sold for $6.50. Soon, with the profits so earned, Astor got rid of the middlemen and entered the shipping business himself to carry his own furs. When his furs were unloaded in London, he would load up his ships with cheap English goods and bring them back to America. In this way, Astor's profits from a single fur, it was said, could stretch to $10.

When he died in 1848, he was the richest man in America, with a fortune estimated at $20 million. There was no one else who even approached this kind of wealth. His estate passed to his son, William Astor, who was 56 at the time of his father's death.

The Astor fortune grew to include other businesses, including banking. The Astors were also aggressive acquirers of land and other real estate. Indeed, while the fur-trade business would eventually cease to be so lucrative and the shipping business would wax and wane, the great bulk of the Astor fortune after the patriarch died came from increases in the value of the family's vast land holdings.

By 1890 the family fortune had swelled to over $150 million. It was estimated that the Astor family real estate holdings on the island of Manhattan alone were worth over $100 million.

There is a telling exchange in testimony over a tax matter before the New York Senate Committee in 1890, in which the Astor fortune is discussed:

Q: You have just said that Mr. Astor never sold?

A: Once in a while he sells, yes.

Q: But the rule is that he does not sell?

A: Well, hardly ever. He has sold, of course.

Q: Isn't it almost a saying in this community that the Astors buy and never sell?

A: They are not looked upon as people who dispose of real estate after they once get possession of it.

The key to the great Astor fortune—what gave it staying power and allowed it to multiply to such extraordinary heights—was the simple fact that the Astors were reluctant sellers. Once they got ahold of a good thing, they held on and allowed the magic of compounding to do its work.

The Astors were not alone in this. The bulk of several tremendous nineteenth-century American fortunes was built by holding on to valuable real estate. The Schermerhorns also built up an impressive fortune by owning tracts of land in New York City. The Longworths owned chunks of Cincinnati when it was but a small outpost of only 800 adventurers. Marshall Field amassed a fortune by holding and developing land in and around Chicago.

There seems to be a great psychological advantage in holding real estate as opposed to holding stocks. People don't sell real estate on a whim, partly because selling real estate is much harder to do than selling stock, which today can be accomplished with a few keystrokes. Also, people don't watch a continuous flow of real estate quotations on a daily basis, as they can and do with stocks. Plus, real estate is something people can see and intuitively understand the value of, more so than with stocks.

As a result, people tend to be much more patient with their real estate than they are with their stocks. But the principles of building wealth are the same in both venues. You have to give the investment time to work for you. And to do that, you must be a reluctant seller. In studying the creation of these great American fortunes, today's investors are indelibly reminded of that fact.

Remember, there are two markets for stocks. Or if you prefer, there are two prices. The quoted price is just one of these two prices, and it shouldn't dominate your decisions. In Chapter 8 of Ben Graham's classic book *The Intelligent Investor,* titled "The Investor and Market Fluctuations," he discusses how investors should react to price changes in their stocks:

> The investor with a portfolio of sound stocks should expect their prices to fluctuate and should neither be concerned by sizable declines nor become excited by sizable advances. He should always remember that market quotations are there for his convenience, either to be taken advantage of or to be ignored. He should never buy a stock *because* it has gone up or sell one *because* it has gone down [italics in the original].[1]

SIMPLE SELL IDEAS

When I met with Ralph Wanger, the famed manager behind the Acorn Fund, he talked about the simple idea behind his sell discipline: You sell when your original reason for owning a stock is no longer true.

This strategy has a long history in finance. It was also used by Phil Fisher, another investment heavyweight in the pantheon of great investors and the author of a number of insightful investment books— notably *Common Stocks and Uncommon Profits.*

Fisher had a very slow trigger finger when it came to selling. He believed that if the job of stock selection was done correctly, the time to sell would be almost never.

He did believe that an investor had to sell when he had made a mistake and "the factual background of the particular company is, by a significant margin, less favorable than originally believed." This idea is similar to Wanger's.

In an interview with *Grant's Interest Rate Observer,* Marty Whitman talks about when to sell: "I've been in this business for over fifty years. I have had a lot of experience holding stocks for three years; doubled, and I sold it for somebody else, for whom it tripled in the next six months. You make more money sitting on your ass."[2]

Whitman, though, also acknowledges times when he sold and wished he sold even more: "We sold a lot of the high-techs early in 2000, and I regretted not having sold much more. It ended up that what we held was a garbage portfolio."[3]

Selling is hard, in part because it's so easy to look like a fool later. Whitman says, "We're just not that smart on the sell side."[4] Few investors, if any, really are. It's nice to hear such candor from one of the best in the business.

"DOLCE FAR NIENTE"

Dolce far niente (pronounced "DOL-chay far nee-EN-tay") is an expression that roughly means, according to William and Mary Morris, "the sweetness of doing nothing." The Morrises put together the *Morris Dictionary of Word and Phrase Origins,* an enjoyable book and great for browsing.

This is a favorite phrase of mine. Try springing it on some poor unsuspecting relatives at dinner tonight. I once used it on my wife to try to get out of some housework. Let's just say I was not wholly successful. I wouldn't advise trying that.

Anyway, it's a good little mantra for investors, especially those who have a hard time sitting on their hands. Inactivity can be a very intelligent thing to do.

I was thinking about this after a reader of the newsletter wrote me a nice letter about the 15 funds that beat Bill Miller's vaunted Value Trust. He noted that all of the funds had a value orientation and also had relatively low amounts of turnover.

Remember Louis Lowenstein from earlier in the book? He wrote a paper years ago that looked at some of the successful value funds in recent years. He found that one common element among them was low turnover. These funds held their investments for years on average.

In sharp contrast, the average mutual fund has a turnover ratio of about 121 percent. This means that the average fund flips its whole portfolio once every ten months on average. That's a lot of activity.

It's similar in football. What statistic correlates best with wins? The turnover ratio. In other words, teams that don't cough up the ball as much as their opponents tend to win. A favorable turnover ratio is a residual—the result of good tackling, protecting the football, making good decisions, and so on. There is a luck element, sure, but over the long haul certain teams maintain better turnover ratios than others.

This reminds me of the University of Maryland's football team in 2006, which had something important to teach investors.

THE TERRAPINS FORMULA

The Terrapins, or Terps as they are affectionately known, were 8–2 and ranked 21st in the country. (In the interest of full disclosure: I'm a Maryland graduate and big fan.) They were in the hunt for their conference's championship. Yet on the surface they seemed to have no business in such a contest.

Their offense and defense didn't crack the top 100. Statistically, they ranked among the dregs of college football. There was an obvious disparity between these facts and their won-loss record. What was going on?

Coach Ralph Friedgen has his own formula for winning. In fact, he's even concocted a new football statistic to measure it. In an interesting story on the team, the *Washington Post* dubbed it "the Terrapins Formula." Friedgen adds up his team's mistakes and divides that total by the number of offensive plays his team ran. These mistakes include penalties, dropped passes, fumbles lost, interceptions, and sacks allowed.

Essentially, he comes up with an error rate that can be expressed in percentages.

Friedgen found that a low error rate—12 percent or less—often leads to victory. He claims a 95 percent accuracy rate over his coaching career. Indeed, over the last two seasons the formula has a 90 percent accuracy rate. In 2006, at least partway through the season, the Terps were 6–0 when their error rate was less than 12 percent.

What's unique about the Terrapins Formula is that it shifts the usual emphasis on scoring to a focus on simply making few mistakes. Most of the time you hear football analysts emphasize points scored or points allowed. Friedgen's measure doesn't take into account any of this. He simply focuses on errors.

The key insight is simple: Make fewer mistakes and you'll win more ball games.

For investors, there is a compelling analogy in all of this. Great investors often talk about paying attention to risks. Warren Buffett, Marty Whitman, Seth Klarman, and others—all focus first on the downside. They first look to answer the question, "How much can I lose?" Only then do they compare how much they could lose with how much they could make.

They want to cover their downside and avoid mistakes (losses). Most average investors don't do this at all. They focus on making gains. They want to know how much they can make.

This is such an important concept—yet so overlooked.

Everyone loses now and then. And sometimes investors lose big. But the idea is that over the long haul you accumulate far more winners and avoid many big losers.

Not exactly the sexiest idea you could have when looking for investments. You can see why *Capital & Crisis,* presenting such dour thoughts, will never be the best-selling newsletter in the world.

Nonetheless, what works works. The Terrapins win ball games because they make few mistakes. And great investors make lots of money for the same reasons, because in certain respects, investing is not so different from football. Low turnover in a portfolio is a result of doing a lot of good fundamental things right. A high turnover ratio implies that an investor has made a lot of mistakes.

Now, I don't think anyone should aim for an arbitrary holding period. You still can't be afraid to change your mind. If it's five months in and you can show you were in error in your analysis, then you shouldn't be afraid to sell. Likewise, sometimes things are out of your control—like when a company gets bought out. But generally speaking, I would say that you should shoot for at least one year out. That seems like a minimum to me.

If you're routinely buying and selling stocks at a quicker pace, then you're not really investing—you're trading, which is a different game altogether. Ideally, of course, you'd like to find a company you can own for many years. Those are rare. I think we have at least a few in my *Capital & Crisis* model portfolio—Brookfield Asset Management, Leucadia, and PICO Holdings immediately come to mind.

This is a short chapter. First, because I've commented on selling in other parts of the book. More importantly, however, it's short because the basic idea of when to sell is easy in principle. It's much tougher in practice, of course. But if you keep the ideas in this chapter in mind, they should help in your decision-making.

CHAPTER 7

ON DOING THE WRONG THING

It is the month of May, in the year 1778. General Washington, holed up in Valley Forge with his ragged Continental Army, has just received intelligence revealing that the British are planning to evacuate Philadelphia.

Washington's response is to send a force across the Schuylkill River to discourage the British from raiding supplies found in the countryside. The damnable Redcoats had already made off with over 2,000 head of sheep and cattle last December. This irritating action had left that much less for the Continental Army, which lived through the winter, not by warm hearths in the city—as the Brits who held Philadelphia did—but out in the chilly wind-whipped countryside.

Washington gives this task to a 19-year-old, red-haired French volunteer, a general who comes from a long line of English-fighting Frenchmen. His own father was cut in half by a cannonball at the Battle of Minden during the Seven Years' War. This French officer, you may have guessed, was the now famous Marquis de Lafayette. This was his first command.

Lafayette led a force of 2,200 men, crossed the river on May 18, and headed for the high ground of nearby Barren Hill. There he set up Enoch Poor's New Hampshire Brigade, the bulk of his force, on high ground next to a Lutheran church, facing south. Allan McLane's Delaware Company, along with 50 Oneida Indians, took up the left flank, along some stone houses on Ridge Road. Steep bluffs along the

Schuylkill protected the right flank. Lafayette sent the 600-man Pennsylvania Militia north to watch the road from Whitemarsh.

Unfortunately for the brave band of revolutionaries, the British had intelligence of their own. The battle-wise Redcoats had lots of fresh, well-fed men and cannons to boot. They had 5,500 men swing north into Whitemarsh, with the plan to attack Lafayette's rear flank. They had another 2,000 men ready to hit his eastern flank on Ridge Road, and yet another 2,000 to meet the Americans at Barren Hill and pin them with their backs to the river.

Moreover, they were aware that Lafayette was leading them. What better way to disgrace the Franco-American alliance than to capture this young aristocrat?

All told, the British had about 10,000 men creating a great pincer to trap Lafayette and his 2,200 men. On May 20, in a foggy dawn, columns of British soldiers made their way up Ridge Road. With smashingly good odds, superior intelligence, and a well-executed plan, they had to be confident in the outcome.

Lafayette, though, was a cagey leader, even at that tender age. He knew he was outnumbered five-to-one, and he had no intention of sticking around. The Continentals had been practicing the art of retreat in countless drills under the Prussian Baron von Steuben at Valley Forge. Now Lafayette put that training to the test.

Lafayette also knew the lay of the land very well. And he knew of another road out—a low, narrow, and rocky road that led to Matson's Ford, where he and his men could scoot back across the river. Lafayette quickly set up flag-bearing columns to make it appear he was ready to engage the enemy.

Meanwhile, he took his main force in an orderly, swift retreat— with his men tightly packed in columns—along the low road, out of the enemy's sight.

By the time the Brits realized what had happened, most of Lafayette's men were already across the river. The Brits caught the tail end of Lafayette's troops at the river crossing, where a small skirmish ensued. Only nine Americans were killed; the British lost two.

So there was no battle here at all, in the usual sense. Instead, it was a battle of wits, which the Americans won decisively, and an important episode for military men, because it showed that the Continentals were emerging as a smart, professional army—one capable of beating the august Redcoats. And it established a high bar for the Revolution's military leadership. The teenage general—facing five-to-one odds—slipped a trap and humiliated Britain's best generals.

What does this have to do with markets? Maybe nothing. Or maybe just this: Where you avoid committing your money is just as important as where you do put it. In other words, invest when the odds are in your favor and avoid those situations when they are not.

Lafayette abandoned Barren Hill to commit his forces when the odds were more favorable. Even in investing, there is room for similar guts and smarts. A few cagey decisions to avoid those areas of the market that will blow up can make all the difference in how well you survive in the stock market over time.

LOOKING FOR AND PAYING FOR GROWTH

As a place to invest, I'll take a lousy industry over a great industry anytime.

—Peter Lynch, Beating the Street

"El Dorado was not originally a place," writes Charles Nicholl in a book called *The Fruit Palace*, "but a person—el dorado, the gilded man."[1] The El Dorado was the king of the fabulous city of Manoa, a place supposedly swimming in gold, where the houses were roofed, and liberally decorated, with the yellow metal. The chieftains of Manoa enjoyed an unusual coronation ceremony that took place in some remote inland lagoon.

"At the shores of the lagoon, he was stripped naked, anointed with sticky resin and sprayed with gold dust. A raft of reeds was prepared, with braziers of moque incense and piles of gold and jewels on it."[2] The chieftain was floated out to the middle of lake, where he then jumped in, washing the gold off his body. The gold and jewels were then dumped in the lake.

When word of this ceremony reached the ears of Spanish explorers, they dreamed of finding the lake and draining it of its hidden riches. English explorers tried to find it, too, including Sir Walter Raleigh.

The city was believed to be located on the Amazon River, or perhaps in the highlands of Colombia. Of course, like other legends, this one became more inaccurate and fantastic in the retellings as bits of other legends and myths were mixed in—so much so that similar myths were heard in the American West and other parts of the world.

Today the words "El Dorado" refer to any mythical place of fabulous wealth or opportunity.

In the stock market, investors, like the Spanish and English explorers of old, are always searching for the stock market equivalent of El Dorado. And the stock market equivalent of the story of El Dorado has also been mixed with bits of legend and myth, such that the real secrets of wealth building became obscured over time. Investors are more prone to believe that finding the next great growth stock in a big, exciting industry is the key to building a great fortune. Not so, says professor Jeremy Siegel.

Siegel's new book, *The Future for Investors,* reminds us that valuations are the critical ingredient to investment returns. While I don't always agree with ever-bullish Siegel, he presents some interesting ideas.

Siegel, a Wharton professor and author of *Stocks for the Long Run* (which, ironically, contributed to much of the myth that stocks at any price are good bets over the long haul), does present some interesting research that shows how some of the best investments of the past half-decade emerged from industries with horrible dynamics. And some of the worst investments have come from the most hyped and popular industries.

Peter Lynch would not be surprised. The quotation at the top of this section indicates that Lynch, like many of the sharpest investors, was on to this idea well before the good professor's book came along. Lynch readily admits that most of his losers came from betting on sexy technology companies in growth industries.

Anecdotally, there are some remarkable contrasts of stocks that did very well in poor industries and stocks that did very badly in so-called good industries.

Among the worst performers, we have no shortage of very recent examples. The communications sector was once the hottest thing going, and its future looked bright. The demand for bandwidth seemed to know no bounds in the 1990s. Internet traffic, it was said, was doubling every 100 days. Technology analysts wrote that no matter how much supply was created, it would be used, and they gave little thought to the idea that there could be a glut of such capacity.

But in fact that's exactly what happened. Leasing a telecom line that carried 150 bytes of data per second cost about $1.6 million in

2000—the peak of the mania. By 2004 it cost about $100,000. Few businesses can survive such a collapse in the pricing of their product.

Keep in mind, too, that this was an industry that raised over three-quarters of a trillion dollars from 1996 to 2000. There was simply no way those investors could ever get their money back—never mind a good return on their investment.

The telecom sector had a market capitalization of about $1.8 trillion at its apex, but collapsed to about $400 million in the bust thereafter. Some call it the most expensive bubble in history.

There are so many examples of companies that collapsed after the bubble peaked—companies still fresh in our memories, like Global Crossing and JDS Uniphase—that they are hardly worth recounting. And it wasn't just telecom—lots of hot sectors in the past have not panned out for investors. In the 1980s, disk drives were the hot item, and analysts forecast growth rates of 50 percent for years. This, in fact, did happen. The problem was that something like 30 companies were competing for the same business, and none of them could make a buck.

In any event, Siegel shows that there have been some real gems in industries that most investors would not have given a second thought to.

An interesting example of this phenomenon occurred in the railroad industry, which Siegel discusses in the book. The railroad industry has been shrinking since the mid-1950s. The creation of a nationwide highway system spurred competition from the trucking industry. And the growth of the airlines ate into the railroads' passenger business. Most people look at the railroads as a dying business, a stagnant, old-world relic.

Siegel's research shows how railroads stocks not only beat out the airlines and trucking industries but even topped the S&P 500 itself. So, despite some bankruptcies and other problems, investors were able to come out well ahead when things improved—even if they improved only a little bit. The history of railroads shows us how an industry in a long decline can still post excellent returns.

There are many other examples, including Southwest in the airline industry and Nucor in steel. The crown, though, must go to Philip Morris, the hated tobacco company. In fact, the best-performing stock in the original S&P 500 (constructed in the mid-1950s) was Philip Morris.

The key point here is that valuations matter. It's not about industry prospects or what the growth rate is. It's not about having positive demographics or supportive macro trends. All of these things can be useful to know and understand, and they can help or hurt an investment in a lot of ways . . . but if you don't consistently buy stocks when they are cheap, these other things are probably not going to save you from subpar returns.

One final example: Siegel puts IBM up against Standard Oil Company of New Jersey (Exxon) in 1950. IBM had better forecast growth rates in revenues, in dividends, and in earnings per share. Moreover, its industry was projected to grow 15 percent per year, while Standard Oil's was projected to decline 14 percent per year. Yet which stock provided the better return from 1950 to 2003? Standard Oil, and it wasn't even close. If you had invested $1,000 in both stocks in 1950, you'd have had $960,000 worth of IBM in 2003 versus about $1.3 million in Exxon. The difference was that IBM traded at much higher valuation multiples than Standard Oil.

Again, it's all about the price you pay. That's your El Dorado, as unglamorous as it seems.

INNOVATIONS ARE NOT ALWAYS IMPROVEMENTS

> *It's such a fine line between stupid and clever.*
> —*David St. Hubbins (played by Michael McKean)*
> *in* This Is Spinal Tap

The following dialogue is from the movie *This Is Spinal Tap* (a "rockumentary" about a fictional British band). The lead guitarist, Nigel Tufnel, is demonstrating the band's amplifiers for interviewer Marty DiBergi. The amplifiers are all fitted with dials that go up to 11 instead of the usual 10:

DiBergi: Does that mean it's louder? Is it any louder?

Tufnel: Well, it's one louder, isn't it? It's not ten. You see, most blokes, you know, will be playing at ten. You're on ten here, all the way up, all the way up, all the way up, you're on ten on your guitar. Where can you go from there? Where?

DiBERGI: I don't know.

TUFNEL: Nowhere. Exactly. What we do is, if we need that extra push over the cliff, you know what we do?

DiBERGI: Put it up to eleven.

TUFNEL: Eleven. Exactly. One louder.

DiBERGI: Why don't you just make ten louder and make ten be the top number and make that a little louder?

TUFNEL: (extremely long pause) These go to eleven.

Innovations are not always improvements, and this is especially true in investing. People are always coming up with seemingly novel ways to make money in the markets. Books come out all the time touting some new way of thinking or some new system. The "newness," however, is more apparent than real.

Most of these new ways just die after a while. There is little that is new in finance. The same principles apply in nearly all markets.

I visited a local used-book shop the other day, looking to sell a box of books I no longer wanted. I didn't care how much they paid me. I just wanted to get rid of them and clear some space on my shelves.

Many of the books were about investing, markets, or economics. As the bookseller picked over the lot, he left many of the investing and economics books in the box and bought the other books.

"I'm always surprised at what you take and don't take," I said to him. "For example, you took a copy of Adam Smith's *Theory of Moral Sentiments,* but you wouldn't take this brand-new book about investing."

This bookseller is a crusty fellow, with a face like a dead squirrel. "Well," he said in a very deliberate manner, "most of what's worth reading about money and investing has already been written."

This was a fairly wise observation, I thought. He continued: "People love to come to a used-book store and pick up copies of the classics that have been around for a hundred years or more. The problem with the new stuff is that we don't know what will stick. What's popular today is forgotten tomorrow."

Yes, that's exactly it. Most of the new stuff is simply putting the dial to 11, as Nigel did, and thinking that makes a difference.

SOSNOFF AND THE FISH THAT NEVER DIE

The new-issue market has as much nobility as the Fulton Fish Market in the noonday sun when the cobblestones are littered with the carcasses of overripe flounder that didn't sell that morning.

—*Martin T. Sosnoff*

I confess that I have a soft spot for old books. Some may think that, in the ephemeral world of finance, old is what happened yesterday and that old means outdated and useless. They would be mistaken. The markets of yesteryear were not so different from markets today, as I was reminded when reading *Humble on Wall Street,* published in 1975.

Money manager and former *Forbes* columnist Martin Sosnoff wrote the book, a memoir of his investing experiences in the '60s and early '70s.

I picked up a tattered copy for $5.95 at a local used-book shop (looking for values, of course). I felt compelled to read it as soon as I saw the dust jacket and came across Sosnoff's quote about the new-issue market. Sosnoff is a graceful writer, and from the beginning he beguiles with his timeless observations of Wall Street.

"As a state of mind," Sosnoff begins in his opening chapter, "Wall Street is no different from Main Street. Lazy and avaricious, prejudiced and easy to panic, it can believe anything and just as readily shed its belief."[3] Wall Street and investors generally have little patience. Their tastes are constantly changing. As a result, cycles have become an unmistakable feature of markets, like the nose on a man's face.

Sosnoff finds an analogy in the art market. He quotes author Gerald Reitlinger: "Sometimes fantasy prices were paid by princes and cardinals alike, like Arab caliphs who filled the mouths of poets with gold. But quite often high prices were reached because two or three magnates wanted the same picture."[4]

It can be years before the prices reached during these bidding frenzies are seen again.

The stock market is not so different. Once, not long ago, it seemed that everyone wanted to own Internet stocks. How long will it be before any of those stocks see their old highs again—if ever? Indeed, many of them no longer exist. At least the princes and cardinals had the pleasure of gazing at their Rubens and Van Dycks, their Rembrandts and Titians.

Optimism is a cheap commodity on Wall Street. There people believe in America every day of the year—and they'll sell it to you for a pretty penny, too!

Optimism permeated the speculative excess of the '60s. Its boom and subsequent bust is the main subject of Sosnoff's memoir. For example, he tells about being a member of a small group of about a dozen speculators who met every month over dinner and talked about their best ideas.

One of these ideas was a plan to raise sweet pompano, a commodity then trading for around two bucks per pound. The fish would be raised cheaply in a controlled environment and sold at a handsome profit. In their roundtable discussions, the speculators could not find fault with the idea and found they were getting very excited about it. In short, they thought they had a sure thing.

Well, they went ahead with their plan, and things seemed to be working perfectly—until the day when the fish inexplicably sickened and died. This, for Sosnoff, was a perfect metaphor for the period. He writes, "None of us had dreamed that the fish could die. This is bull market thinking—the fish never die." But the fish do die, as Sosnoff points out, and the market becomes "a surrealistic canvas of fantasies from old cycles superimposed on the new realities." The urge to get rich quick never goes away.[5]

In the '60s, growth investing was in style, and investors used all kinds of assumptions to rationalize stratospheric price-earnings multiples. Wall Street, "the personification of positive thinking through numbers juggling . . . suffers from the tyranny of a thousand slide rule pushers who lack the imagination and courage to soar above facts and focus on circumstance."[6] Today slide rule pushers have given way to pushers of Excel spreadsheets, but they're still practicing intellectual tyranny all the same.

When Virginia Electric Power, a utility company, was trading at 27 times earnings in the '60s, there was no shortage of numbers justifying its performance—numbers that were subsequently ruined by the realities of rising financing and soaring fuel costs. Perspective is what numbers men lacked then and still lack today.

Analysts are overly optimistic in their forecasts during good times and overly pessimistic in bad times, creating opportunities for investors brave enough to buck the consensus. As Sosnoff points out, analysts "will refuse to put their names to anything controversial at the bottom of a cycle. This is the meat for the conceptualist who is strong enough to anticipate the facts by maybe six months."[7]

From this, Sosnoff postulates a law that is both funny and true, at least in my experience: "The price of a stock varies inversely with the thickness of its research file."[8] In other words, fat research files generally mean you were able to find loads of information on the company—and hence are probably too late. Think about it. Large blue chips are no secret, and research on those companies is easy. Digging for information on smaller, lesser-known opportunities is much harder.

It would also be wise to avoid new issues, or initial public offerings. Usually heavily promoted, they are speculations at best. Symbolically, they show that, as Sosnoff notes, "there always is a new generation coming along willing to live by the sword and die by the sword for the greater glory and greed of nobody but No. 1. These boys are content to breathe only pure oxygen on the frontier of speculation."[9]

Bear markets have a way of turning dreams into nightmares. I think it was Emerson who wrote that nature pardons no errors. The market can be similarly unforgiving. The 1973–1974 bear market took the growth investing mania of the '60s to the woodshed. Those sky-high multiples came crashing down. Stocks started to trade like bonds. Instead of 30 to 40 times earnings, companies were trading for 6 times earnings. If you were a particularly unpopular conglomerate (once adored in the '60s), you might find your stock trading for 4 times earnings.

Stocks were reviled in 1973–1974. Pension funds, in the fall of 1973, only gingerly put new money in stocks. It was a trickle not seen in over a decade. At the exact moment when stocks were cheapest, investors took a pass. What was hot in 1973? Bonds! At the moment when buying bonds was the worst thing to do (the inflationary '70s would inflict deep losses on bondholders), investors snapped them up.

Reliably, the mass of investors did the wrong thing. They can be counted on to do the wrong thing again.

BEDROCK CONTRARIAN INSIGHTS

The bedrock contrarian insight is simply that it is time to be careful whenever the mass of investors gets excited about an idea—because the masses are usually late to the ball, and their arrival tends to signal the imminent 12th hour, when Cinderella's carriage turns back into a pumpkin.

In an attempt to uncover the next great bubble, investors have created numerous contrarian indicators. Some of these are more amusing and colorful than useful. There are indicators built around magazine covers, best-selling books, and Alan Abelson's columns. Whatever premise is being pitched from these sources, the theory goes, you would be wise to not follow the advice.

There are exceptions, of course, which makes following these things all the more problematic. Plus, to continue with the Cinderella analogy, there is no clock that strikes midnight at the appointed hour. As investors, we are left to guess. And guess we do.

Another indicator might be based on the chatter you hear at investment conferences. We might call this the "Bemelmans Bellhop Indicator," in honor of author Ludwig Bemelmans, who is best known for his children's stories about the little girl named Madeleine (who lives in an "old house in Paris all covered with vines"). But he also wrote several lively stories about the happenings in and around hotels and restaurants during the heady 1920s. These were collected in a book titled *Hotel Bemelmans,* republished in 2004. In one of the stories, a Mr. von Kyling sells out his position in the market after hearing the enthusiasm with which other hotel employees are investing in the market.

I thought of von Kyling while I was in Vancouver in 2005 for the Agora Wealth Symposium, held at the beautiful downtown Fairmont Hotel. While there, I heard a lot of enthusiastic talk about China, including from my cabbie. It seems that it was the main thing most investors wanted to talk about. China headlines sell. People flock to hear about investing in China. Could this also be a warning sign?

It could be. But more interesting is what people were not talking about. At a conference about global investing, I heard quite a bit about China and India and even Brazil. I also heard a lot of talk about energy and the dollar.

No one was talking about Mexico.

I steered my readers to Mexico in late 2004, and it wound up as the third-best-performing market that year (2005), behind only South Korea and Brazil, among Dow Jones World Index countries.

Among the worst was China.

In fact, it would surprise most people to discover that China's stock market was among the worst performers in the world for several years running. One year the Shanghai benchmark index dropped 15 percent, even though the economy continued to grow, making China's stock market the worst-performing market among the world's major markets. Despite rapid economic growth and over 513 new listings since 2000, the total market capitalization of China's stock market was about one-third less by 2005.

There are a lot of problems with China's market. Still, the point is that while investors were pining for China investment ideas and the economy seemed to be booming, the underlying performance of those investments, for the most part, was poor.

And what about Mexico?

On a long plane ride, I read a book titled *Dictionary Days* by Mexican-born author Ilan Stavans, now an American citizen. There is a passage in the book where he ruminates on a day spent revisiting his native land. He writes about attending a play and seeing a poor Indian woman sitting on the ground. Dressed in traditional embroidered regalia, the woman had long, unkempt hair and a bronze, wrinkled face. Around her was a colorful display of merchandise for sale: Mayan folklore dolls, sweet-and-spicy candy, Chiclets, Japanese peanuts, and other assorted souvenirs and gifts.

The woman served as a reminder, Stavans writes, that "Mexico's modernity is still unfinished business . . . although the government lavishly promotes the idea that, as Octavio Paz put it once, 'Mexico has finally joined the banquet of Western civilization,' the truth is otherwise: A large portion of the population still cannot spell the word yo."[10]

So I am not denying that Mexico is still a largely poor country with its share of emerging-market pains. But at a certain price it becomes worth the risk. I would argue that if you do the micro work well, the macro stuff becomes less important (think of micro as the gritty details of companies and specific investments, and macro as the bigger picture of industries and economies). Cheap valuations, or a margin of safety, will pull you through a lot of adversity, just like a St. Bernard dog pulls travelers from Alpine snowdrifts.

Interestingly enough, I came upon an old lecture delivered by historian Lord Acton (author of the maxim "Power tends to corrupt, and absolute power tends to corrupt absolutely") in 1868 entitled "The Rise and Fall of the Mexican Empire." Here is a snippet, which is intriguing because of its essential timelessness:

> The scene of the tragedy which I will attempt to describe is a country on which Nature's fairest gifts have been lavished with an unsparing hand, but where man has done his utmost to thwart the designs of Providence. . . . Mexico possesses a territory more than thrice as large as France, with the fertility of the tropics, and the climate of the temperate zone, seated between two oceans, in the future center of the commerce of the world. Its wealth in precious metals is so enormous that the time will come when the market will be flooded with silver, and its price will not allow the mines to be worked with profit.[11]

Certain lands and places always seem to capture the imagination. Investors' favorites just seem to rotate around; Brazil, India, and Russia—to name a few—have all had some time in the limelight in recent years. But it is often better to fish around where there are fewer fishermen. In other words, look at markets that are not now in the headlines.

In *Capital & Crisis,* I wrote a bullish profile of Japan in early 2004 and made a pair of recommendations on that theme. Japan's shares subsequently hit four-year highs—despite a drumbeat of worry and negativity about deflation, demographics, debts, and other woes. Again, at a certain price, Japanese stocks become worth playing.

China is a hot story, no doubt, and the emergence of China is having a dramatic impact on the patterns of global trade. Yet investors would probably do better to resist the obvious and instead look for other avenues to pursue and other ways to invest. To continue with the Cinderella theme, look for the mice that have not yet turned into horses, and the pumpkins that have not yet become carriages.

THINGS ARE SELDOM WHAT THEY SEEM

It is an important and popular fact that things are not always what they seem. For instance, on the planet Earth, man had always assumed that he was more intelligent than dolphins because he had achieved so much—the wheel, New York, wars and so on—while all the dolphins had ever done was muck about in the water having a good time. But conversely, the dolphins had always believed that they were far more intelligent than man—for precisely the same reasons.
　　—*Douglas Adams,* The Hitchhiker's Guide to the Galaxy [12]

The Hitchhiker's Guide to the Galaxy series of books was popular in the 1980s. It is nominally a work of science fiction but can more accurately be described as a timeless piece of light comedy, in the tradition of the great P. G. Wodehouse. Wodehouse wrote comic novels and short stories that involved English cottages and stately manors in a world filled with servants and men of leisure. Adams's comic tales take place in a world of space travel, aliens, and incredibly intelligent mice. (On Adams's twisted Earth, man is the third-most-intelligent creature on the planet, right after the dolphins. The mice are on top: "The whole business with the cheese and the squeaking is just a front," he writes.)

One of Adams's creations is a race of beings that manufacture custom-made planets, a very expensive luxury item, as you might have guessed. When the Galactic economy collapses, so does their market. But they devise an interesting way to weather the storm: "The recession came, and we decided it would save us a lot of bother if we just slept through it," explains one of the characters.[13]

They program a computer to revive them when the recession blows over. "The computers were index-linked to the Galactic stock market prices, you see, so that we'd all be revived when everybody else had rebuilt the economy enough to afford our rather expensive services," he continues.[14]

Of course, we can't sleep through a tough market. In fact, as value investors, we don't want to, because it is during such times of general unrest that we may be able to uncover some real bargains.

In truth, *The Hitchhiker's Guide to the Galaxy* has nothing to do with investing, at least not without a great deal of stretching. I pulled out my copy because I saw a trailer advertising a soon-to-be-released movie based on the book and was curious enough to read it again. Anyway, the book is a light read, and you could probably finish it in a few hours. It is great fun—if you're into that sort of thing. And it offers the occasional gem. (Here is one more: "He felt his whole life was some kind of dream, and he sometimes wondered whose it was and whether they were enjoying it."[15])

But maybe *The Hitchhiker's Guide* is not as irrelevant to investing as I first thought. The book's philosophical subtext is that the universe is a very large place, enormously complex, full of surprises, and tough to figure out. The characters in the book find themselves often befuddled and frustrated. The financial markets are a lot like this.

When I was at a Grant's Investment Conference once, the luncheon speaker was Emanuel Derman, a former director of Goldman Sachs and now a Columbia University professor, as well as the author of a terrific memoir titled *My Life as a Quant: Reflections on Physics and Finance*. His book and his speech both deal with the puzzle that markets present.

Derman, a physicist by training, came to Wall Street to work as a quantitative financial analyst (or "quant"). As a quant, he worked to build mathematical models that traders could use profitably and reliably, though he quickly came to realize the futility of what he was doing. The techniques of physics and the hard sciences simply don't work well in the world of finance. There are few financial truths in the sense that there are truths in physics—such as models that predict the future trajectories of planets with accuracy or that predict the properties of new particles. Mathematical models cannot capture the unpredictability of human psychology.

This fact leads to all sorts of revelations, both wise and humorous. One of them deals with Paul Wilmott, a mathematician, who wrote a book on derivatives called *Wilmott on Derivatives*. As Derman observes, "True science does not need that kind of authority—one cannot imagine a 1918 textbook called 'Einstein on Gravitation'!" That's because the theory of gravitation earns its stripes based on its ability to predict real-world phenomena and on its irresistible arguments. "Personality plays a larger role in economic writing," Derman notes, "because truth's part is smaller."[16]

There are other amusing anecdotes and bits of wisdom in the book. For instance, Derman experiences what he describes as "ambition's degradation." He writes that at 17 he wanted to be another Einstein. By the time he was 21 he would have been happy to be another Feynman. "By 1976, sharing an office with other postdoctoral researchers at Oxford, I realized that I had reached the point where I merely envied the postdoc in the office next door because he had been invited to give a seminar in France."[17]

This is a wonderful book, and I highly recommend it to those with an interest in high finance and the puzzles it provides.

MORE ON CYCLES, BOOMS, AND BUSTS

Vancouver played host to the Agora Wealth Symposium in 2004, where I was a speaker and an attendee. I stayed at the Fairmont Hotel in downtown Vancouver, where my room provided a terrific view of the harbor down Burrard Street and overlooked a marvelous 115-year-old cathedral on Georgia Street.

Like most cities, Vancouver's history brings together disparate elements. It is the home of Botox inventor Dr. Jean Carruthers, and it's also the city where Greenpeace was founded in 1971. While I was there, the history of the place seemed to reach back out of the past and spread itself on the nation's newspapers. The market has no special regard for history, as the travails of the Hudson's Bay Company attest.

Hudson's Bay Company was then a 334-year-old department store chain. It was Canada's oldest company. While this advanced age certainly deserves respect and inspires wonder, it seems to buy you no quarter in the rough-and-tumble world of making money.

Hudson's Bay Company was struggling, and the papers reported that the tired old merchant had had enough and might be sold. Target and investor Jerry Zucker were competing suitors to buy the company.

This fact, of course, fanned the burning embers of patriotism in Canada, as they lamented the passing of such a venerable institution. Hudson's Bay was the last great domestic department store since 133-year-old Eatons failed in 1999.

Vancouver's history is also intertwined with that of Hudson's Bay. It was Hudson's Bay explorers who, in the summer of 1827, built a fur-trading post on the banks of the Fraser River, calling it Fort Langley. Colonel Richard Moody arrived from England in 1858 and proceeded to move the post further downstream. Then, coveting an ocean view, he moved it again to Burrard Inlet.

It was a wise choice apparently, as trade and settlement flourished in the area. By 1887 the Canadian Pacific Railway was bringing people to the newly minted city of Vancouver.

Today Vancouver seems to be a prosperous city, with sleek, modern buildings standing beside older, noble ones, with busy streets and shops and people hustling about town. The Hudson's Bay Company store I saw seemed busy enough.

Markets change, though, and while Hudson's Bay Company has been a loser, such things don't usually persist forever. Just as periods of high returns invite competition and put pressure on future returns, so, too, do poor returns tend to rebound as market forces correct the error. Target may have been able to do better with Hudson's assets.

This theme of the cyclical nature of returns was the topic of one of my speeches at the symposium.

ONLY DEAD FISH SWIM WITH THE STREAM

Most people want to buy strong companies with growing sales and expanding markets and a bright future. No one wants to buy a company that has problems to work through, that has been hit with one setback or another, or that has a murky and uninviting outlook in the short term.

Yet it is in these latter opportunities that the greatest investors have plied their trade and milled their fortunes. Warren Buffett bought the *Washington Post* in the throes of the 1973–1974 bear market, when it was struggling. He bought 10 percent of the company for about $10 million. At the time the company had revenues of over $200 million. Ten years later Buffett's stake was worth $250 million.

He bought GEICO when, in his words, "it wasn't essentially bankrupt, but it was heading there." It was one of his greatest acquisitions.

Not just Buffett but scores of wealthy investors have enjoyed incredible returns by buying when other investors were fearful and by seeing through the temporary setbacks.

The greatest investors did not fear to go against the consensus. As writer Malcolm Muggeridge used to say, "Only dead fish swim with the stream."

The paradoxical nature of market returns was brought to light in a book titled *Capital Account: A Money Manager's Reports from a Turbulent Decade, 1993–2002* and edited by Edward Chancellor (author of the acclaimed *Devil Take the Hindmost*). The book collects financial reports written by Marathon Asset Management's partners and delivered to its clients over the boom years. Marathon is an investment advisory firm based in London that manages over $24 billion in assets for institutional investors.

The book is interesting because it illustrates Marathon's unconventional investment style and provides a number of useful ideas and examples of investments that succeeded by bucking consensus opinion.

Consider General Dynamics, a company that Marathon backed in the early 1990s. General Dynamics was in bad shape at the time, suffering from a declining backlog of business in the wake of the Soviet Union's demise.

New management took the company in a different direction in 1991 by closing or selling unprofitable businesses and buying back its own depressed shares.

The stock of General Dynamics increased sixfold between 1990 and 1993 even though its sales were reduced by half.

Yes, sales declined by 50 percent and the stock rose sixfold!

Marathon used the example to highlight a couple of key points regarding its "capital cycle approach" (which I'll get to in a minute). First, investment returns can have less to do with sales and growing markets than with the efficient allocation of resources.

In this case, the management of General Dynamics took the existing resources of the company and dramatically changed the way those resources were deployed. Instead of frittering resources away on unprofitable business lines, management focused on its core business. Even though this involved effectively making the business smaller, investors were rewarded with an outsized gain in the stock price during a relatively short amount of time.

Second, Marathon pointed out that General Dynamics benefited from a decline in competition, as money was withdrawn from the defense sector or diverted to other areas and the existing businesses consolidated. As Chancellor writes, "It is better to invest in a mature industry where competition is declining than in a growing industry where competition is expanding."

Marathon's "capital cycle approach" is based on a simple yet compelling idea. High returns on capital, or the prospect of high returns on capital in one area of the market, attract additional investment. This additional investment puts downward pressure on returns in that market.

Think about the Internet bubble. When the Internet was still new, the first few firms in the space commanded large market caps relative to the amount of capital invested in the business or the amount of money required to start the business. As a result, more money kept pouring into dot-com businesses.

Let me give you Chancellor's distillation of this idea, and you will never forget it.

He wrote, "When a hole in the ground costs $1 to dig but is priced in the stock market at $10, the temptation to reach for a shovel becomes irresistible."[18]

Using the capital cycle approach, you would become suspicious when shares are priced on the assumption that existing returns are going to be maintained or improved in light of rapidly expanding new investment and growing capacity in a business or industry. In other words, the approach helps guard against the error of simply extrapolating prior returns into future years. The capital cycle approach forces you to think about competitive pressures.

The process works in reverse as well. As share prices decline, investment capital moves off to find greener pastures and competition declines. As excess capacity is sweated off, though, returns are likely to improve. Here is where opportunity lies, as share prices in these situations are often priced assuming the pessimistic present conditions are permanent. But as things improve and the market naturally adjusts, these companies may provide outsized returns for far-seeing investors. General Dynamics did exactly that. Target may be able to do that with Hudson's Bay.

HEDGE FUNDS: HISTORY SAYS MORE BLOWUPS ON THE WAY

Leon Cooperman is one of those tough eggs from the Bronx. As a successful investor for over 40 years, he's made more money in markets than most people will ever see in their entire lifetimes. He's witnessed many cycles, watched Wall Street's passions run hot and cold, and endured all the calamities the market could muster over that time span. And he's still playing the game successfully today.

Guys like him start to take on a certain aura. Other investors defer to the old fellow, as American patriots may have looked upon an old soldier who walked the ramparts at Bunker Hill and fired muskets at Lexington and Concord.

So it was with attentive ears that the audience listened to what Cooperman had to say as he addressed the throng at Columbia University. Though his talk touched on many topics, I enjoyed his perspective on the current hedge fund boom. Cooperman presented a fairly damning piece of history that does not bode well for these hedge funds—or their investors.

Hedge funds, to back up a bit, are like mutual funds without some of the restraints. They are often leveraged, sometimes dangerously so. The most notable feature of a hedge fund, though, is its compensation structure. Typically, hedge fund managers get 2 percent of assets managed and 20 percent of any profits generated. That's quite a take.

This is why so many hedge fund managers live in swanky neighborhoods in Connecticut and have vacation homes in exclusive addresses like Martha's Vineyard. It's been said that hedge funds are not an investment but a compensation scheme.

In any case, investors seem to love them—taken by the glamour perhaps, or subdued by visions of big brains cranking out a steady stream of riches using complex systems. Whatever the reason, hedge funds are popular. Assets under the management of the hedge fund industry totaled $1.2 trillion at the end of the second quarter of 2006, according to Hedge Fund Research Inc. That's nearly double the total of only three years earlier. Many expect assets to top $2 trillion over the next couple of years (see Figure 7.1).

The total number of hedge funds in the market is around 9,000. J. Carlo Cannell, the witty and highly successful money manager behind Cannell Capital, recently noted that there are more hedge funds than Taco Bells in the United States. Indeed, there are more hedge funds than publicly traded stocks.

Perhaps handing over such lucrative compensation would be tolerable if said hedge funds delivered the goods.

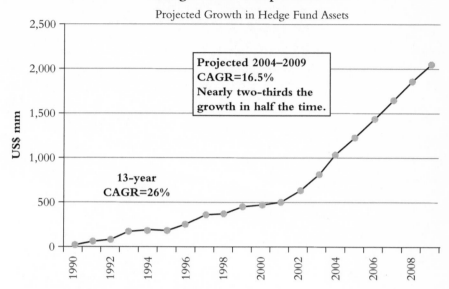

Hedge Funds—People Love 'Em

Projected Growth in Hedge Fund Assets

> **Projected 2004–2009**
> **CAGR=16.5%**
> **Nearly two-thirds the**
> **growth in half the time.**

13-year
CAGR=26%

FIGURE 7.1   Hedge Funds—People Love 'Em

Source: Celene Communications

Yet performance has been mediocre. The average hedge fund rose 13 percent in 2006, lagging behind the 13.6 percent increase of the S&P 500 index. Why pay all that money to hedge fund managers when you can do better in an index fund?

The lackluster performance continues a trend of the last few years as hedge funds have lagged the market (see Figure 7.2).

Not that this is the end-all of analysis. (There are plenty of problems with the hedge fund index that I won't get into here.) And this doesn't mean that there aren't some hedge funds out there worth every bit of the extra money. But it does cause you to rethink the whole boom a bit, doesn't it?

You'll see from Figure 7.2 that hedge funds had their shining moment in the market meltdown following the 2000 peak. Perhaps because of this, investors think of them as bulletproof.

But Cooperman reminded the audience that hedge funds historically have a high casualty rate, despite the fact that the name "hedge

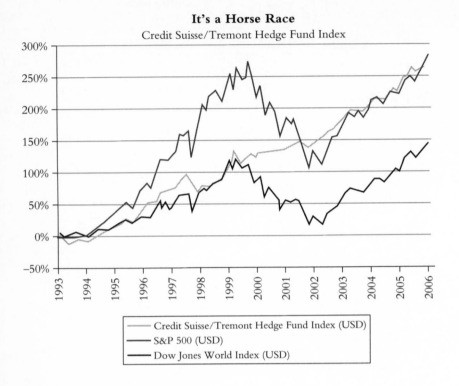

It's a Horse Race

FIGURE 7.2   It's a Horse Race

fund" implies some sort of hedging against risks. Take a look at Table 7.1, which shows the largest hedge funds in 1968—the last time, according to Cooperman, that investors were so in love with the concept. Look what happened to them in the subsequent market downturn.

It's an ugly picture. Somehow I think the current hedge fund boom will end with similar casualties. Human beings circa 2007 are not so different from the 1968 model.

To some extent, it is already happening, as new hedge funds crop up every month to take the place of their fallen comrades. The managers of a busted hedge fund often just open shop again under a new corporate name. The founder of the failing Amaranth Fund, Nick Maounis, has promised to return to the hedge fund world. No doubt, he will find investors.

The now infamous Amaranth, in case you missed it, blew up in late 2006 and early 2007. The firm made big bets on natural gas. It did so at eight-to-one leverage, meaning it borrowed $8 for every $1 of its

TABLE 7.1 Hedge Fund Casualties, December 31, 1968, through September 30, 1970

Hedge Fund	Gain (Loss)
A. W. Jones & Co.	(86%)
City Associates	(78%)
Fleschner Becker Associates	(80%)
Fairfield Partners	(56%)
Cerberus Associates	(55%)
Steinhardt Fine Berkowitz	(5%)
Strand & Co.	(67%)
Lincoln Partners	(1%)
Hawthorn Associates	(73%)
Boxwood Associates	(54%)
Whitehall Associates	(77%)
Woodpark Associates	(100%)
Garente Harrington Associates	(73%)
Scruggs & Co.	(66%)
Broad Street Partners	(64%)
Berger Kent Associates	(94%)
Tamarack Associates	(93%)
Hartwell & Associates	(87%)
Buttonwood Associates	(100%)

own money it put in. Using this kind of leverage is like playing with matches around gasoline tanks. When natural gas prices collapsed, the firm took a big hit.

I'm not sure what the final loss was, but reports indicate it was more than 65 percent. Amaranth had about $9 billion in assets at the time. That's $6 billion in losses if you are keeping score at home.

Amaranth now takes its place on a long list of blown-up hedge funds from years past. There will certainly be more. "If there is one Amaranth, you don't have to be a master sleuth to suspect there are others," wrote Seth Klarman in his annual letter.[19] Klarman is the genius investor behind Baupost's spectacular record. On the matter of hedge funds, he and Cooperman find themselves on the same side, like bluecoats standing shoulder to shoulder at Yorktown. Klarman calls hedge funds "informational black holes." As with Las Vegas, what happens at a hedge fund stays at the hedge fund. Investors in these funds have little way of knowing what risks the fund is taking.

Cooperman offered up his advice to the eager ears at Columbia U. Taking a shot at the perceived brashness and relative youth of the hedge fund universe, Cooperman prescribed a heavy dose of the basic blocking and tackling of finance: "You're better off studying companies. Understand accounting and how businesses work . . . before you become a master of the universe."[20]

Investors who want to be around when the cycle turns will take note.

THE MAN WHO BROKE THE BANK AT MONTE CARLO

The following story comes to us from the annals of gambling, but it holds an important lesson for investors and speculators alike.

Arriving from England on July 19, 1891, Charles Deville Wells went to Monte Carlo to gamble. He was, in the words of author Max Gunther, "a short, fat, rather mysterious Englishman with an obscure background as a freelance inventor and speculator."[21] Wells's favorite game was roulette, and on this trip his exploits would pass into legend.

With about 100,000 francs in his pocket, he hit the roulette tables. After 11 hours of play, he had turned his 100,000-franc stake into 250,000 francs. He was playing red/black and even/odd and hitting his spots with uncanny accuracy, drawing a crowd of onlookers who watched in amazement.

He "broke the bank" that day, which meant simply that the table reached its limit for losses and had to close down for the evening. In those days, a casino would drape the table with a black cloth and dramatically proclaim the table was broke. It was good publicity for the casino, and when the table was reopened, gamblers would flock to that table, perhaps out of some superstitious belief that there was something "wrong" with it. Breaking the bank was a rare occurrence, needless to say, as the casino's tables did not often take such big hits, especially since the odds so heavily favored the house.

But Wells wasn't finished. He went back two nights later and returned to the same table. This time he placed riskier bets by picking groups of numbers instead of playing the red/black, even/odd games. The odds against the player were far greater, but the payoffs were larger.

"As a hushed and startled crowd watched," Gunther writes, "Wells proceeded to break the bank a second time."[22] Casino detectives watched his every move, inspected the wheel, and questioned the croupiers. But they could find no wrongdoing or evidence of foul play.

Wells now began to enjoy some measure of fame. He was courted by high society—beautiful women, millionaires, and noblemen. They all hoped to learn the secrets of his success. Fred Gilbert wrote a song called "The Man Who Broke the Bank at Monte Carlo," which became a hit in April 1892. Bands would play it whenever he walked into a nightclub.

Wells, too, began to live it up. He was often found dressed in top hat and tails. He boldly proclaimed that anyone could watch him play and feel free to imitate him, but he felt most gamblers lacked courage. He would pontificate to all who would listen about how you can't be afraid to bet big and you can't be afraid of losses.

Wells played up the fact that he had a system. He was an engineer and inventor, he would remind his listeners, and the idea for his moneymaking system came to him when he was working out a new fuel-saving device for steamships.

Wells was still not done. In fact, his greatest feat was yet to come. In the winter of 1892, he sailed for Monte Carlo again, aboard an exquisite yacht, the *Palais Royal,* which boasted a dance floor, a music room, and accommodation for 60 guests.

Once in Monte Carlo, he headed for the roulette tables. This time he played the riskiest bet of all—he put his money on single numbers. On the old roulette wheels, there were 36 numbers, plus a zero for the house. Therefore, the odds were 37–1 against anyone picking single numbers. But if you won, you got your money back plus 35 times that amount.

As Gunther writes, "It is a high-risk, high-payoff game, one for people who have nerves of steel, or have a lot of unwanted money or are drunk."[23]

Wells walked in, put his money on the number 5 . . . and left it there. The number 5 came up five times in a row, and he broke the bank . . . again! He pocketed something like half a million francs, which was a fortune in those days.

It would prove to be the apex of Wells's career. Shortly thereafter, he began to lose . . . and lose . . . and lose . . . and lose some more.

Soon he was wiring his rich friends in London for money, which he then promptly lost. Then he accumulated insurmountable debts, leading to his arrest and a three-year term in prison. Once released, Wells would continue to play the role of confidence man, and he would continue to get in trouble in other shady ventures.

In 1926 "The Man Who Broke the Bank at Monte Carlo" died broke in Paris. And what of his system? Wells admitted he had no system. He had just enjoyed a terrific lucky streak. The only real winner was the casino: it eventually got all of its money back from Wells, and the resulting publicity brought lots of new gamblers to Monte Carlo.

Now, dear reader, we bring the thing round to investing.

In investing, it can be hard to determine who is lucky and who really has something that works. There are lots of stock pickers out there who have runs of winning stock picks. But the results don't necessarily mean they are great stock pickers. They could simply be lucky.

Anyone can compile a short-term record of excellence. Luck can play a large role in short-term investment results. Moreover, stellar short-term results are not often sustainable or replicable. Investors should seek a style that has worked over a longer period of time in a variety of markets.

The problem with the Wells episode was that people had a hard time believing he was simply lucky. They had to rationalize in their minds what he had done; they had to attribute it to some "system." In the world of equities, we often do the same thing. Some money manager gets hot and compiles a wonderful three-year (or less) track record, and everyone wants to anoint this manager the next guru. We must remember that it is possible he or she was simply lucky. There are thousands of money managers and thousands of stock pickers, and it is not unusual to expect that several will be hot for no reason other than luck.

The investment style or philosophy of the investor can give us clues, too, especially when we don't have a long track record to evaluate. Ask yourself: Is there a system or style here that is consistent and makes sense?

During the Internet boom a number of mutual funds, for example, compiled outrageous track records speculating in Internet stocks. This was an instance of simply being in a hot market, and most of these funds did not have a real underlying investment thesis to back them up. They picked Internet stocks because they were Internet stocks, not because of any special investment insights. There was nothing behind them; they were just like Wells and his roulette wheel gambles.

What I take from the story of Wells's adventures is that you can have extraordinary runs of luck, good or bad, that are unexplainable in terms of any system that might reproduce such results consistently. In investing, there are plenty of people with results that do not reflect the underlying merits of their approach.

But we have to pay attention to the how and why of those results. Because, as Wells found out, in the long run all these things will get sorted out and the phonies will be exposed.

CHAPTER 8

SMALL QUESTIONS, BIG OPPORTUNITIES

Apparently, a lot of viet kieu (overseas Vietnamese) and their partners are becoming rather wealthy on the unofficial recycling of trash and garbage, prompting, it is said, one Central Committee member to muse chidingly, "We—all of us—always ask only the big questions. It took just one foreigner to ask a small question: Where does the garbage go?"

—Anthony Bourdain, *The Nasty Bits*[1]

Television and radio and the free dailies thrash out the big questions. Everyone has an opinion. Answers to the big macro questions are mostly free. They're given away because few people will pay for them. And there's a good reason for that: It's the answers to the small questions that make the money.

Most people don't know that famed economist John Maynard Keynes (pronounced "Canes") was actually a fairly accomplished investor. Even though I loathe the snarl of ideas he unleashed on the realm of economics, he had some interesting things to say about investing. As the steward of King's College's endowment from 1928 to 1945—a difficult set of years, given the Great Depression sandwiched in between—he managed an average return of 13.2 percent. This looks especially sweet considering that the overall market in the United Kingdom actually lost money during those years, declining by an average of 0.5 percent per year.

Keynes's basic philosophy was to buy cheap, out-of-favor invest-ments, hold on for a period of years, and concentrate the portfolio in his best ideas—as opposed to buying a little bit of lots of ideas.

Keynes's contrarian investment style could be difficult to imple-ment. He had to get his ideas past an investment committee. Investing, I believe, is something that can't be done well by committee. It is best to have one guy make the ultimate decisions.

Anyway, this committee, like all committees, was more interested in showing off what it knew and protecting its behind. This led to some humorous exchanges between Keynes and the committee, which Bill Miller (the manager of Legg Mason Value Trust) recently retold at an investment conference in New York.

Keynes once recommended Argentine bonds. The committee nixed the idea, essentially saying the outlook for Argentina was no good. That response prompted the witty Keynes to reply:

> I want to again explain my investment philosophy. It's called con-trarianism. And what that means is that the stuff I like is stuff that the average person, when they look at it, won't like, and, indeed, will think it imprudent. So the fact the committee doesn't like it is the best evidence for it being a good investment.

On another occasion, the market was falling apart, and the com-mittee asked him if he should be reducing his exposure. Keynes wrote back: "I wouldn't consider it imprudent to own a few shares at the bottom of the market. Your apparent investment approach is that I should be liquidating as the market gets more attractive, and that I should be buying as it goes up."

My favorite Keynesian line is about taking losses. He wrote: "I consider it the duty of every serious investor to suffer grievous losses with great equanimity."

Unfortunately, Keynes wasn't content to be solely an investor, or perhaps the batty committee drove him to look for other things to do. Either way, he wrote an incoherent blob of a book that soon became the new bible of economics. His ideas became the basis of a new highly mathematical approach to economics, which encouraged big government spending and active management of the economy. That's a topic for another place.

DON'T PANIC WHEN YOUR STOCKS FALL

For most people, when a stock they own is down, they get nervous. They think about selling.

Most people are not dealmakers.

For the true dealmaker, market prices are just that—market prices. They are not well-reasoned appraisals of business value. They are the product of opinion and emotion and can be way off base. They are there to take advantage of or ignore, as the case may be.

True dealmakers don't try to time the market. They don't trade stocks. They don't look for insights from chart patterns or recent market action. Stop-losses (traders mechanically looking to sell if stocks fall to certain levels) are not even part of their language.

The investors who understand this live a good life. Not only is their investment performance generally better over the long term, but they just don't worry as much. They are secure in their knowledge and their research. They are calm and reflective, even when the market is turbulent and pulsing with fear.

They spend time away from their computer screens. They sleep well at night, as the old saying goes.

Your investment dollars are safest in cash. That is true. Yet there is an old saying: "Ships are safest in the harbor, but that's not what ships are built for." If you are really a long-term investor, you ought to welcome the lower prices as a chance to pick up some choice bargains.

LOOK AROUND IN AWARENESS

Let us not look back in anger, nor forward in fear, but around in awareness.

—James Thurber, American writer

One time when I was in New York I had dinner at Sushi Samba, which bills itself as a blend of Brazilian and Japanese cuisine. Seems like an odd combination. Japan and Brazil are on opposite sides of the globe. But as it turns out, Brazil is home to the largest population of Japanese people outside of Japan.

A unique swirl of cultural, economic, and legal forces created this interesting mix. In the early twentieth century, exclusion acts all but ended legal immigration from Asia to the United States. Brazil, on the other hand, needed labor for its booming coffee plantations. So Japanese workers facing poor prospects in Japan headed there.

Then, in the 1980s, the story shifted. The Brazilian economy stalled, and the migration wave shifted back to Japan. The tide was so large that the Japanese government issued special visas for those who could prove they were of Japanese descent.

These people of Japanese descent brought much of the Brazilian culture they had absorbed back to Japan with them. This created little Brazils in Japanese cities, like Chinatowns in the United States. And this, in turn, attracted even more of the Brazilian element. There are now over 250,000 Brazilians working in Japan.

I don't know what the investment implications of this are. There may be none. But these odd connections always fascinate me. Successful long-term investing is about more than just finding cheap stocks. It's about finding those little connections that the market doesn't yet see or appreciate. It's about understanding why something may be cheap and seeing how the market could be wrong.

Sometimes these connections involve unique cultural and social evolutions or small twists of fate at the intersections of history and economics. Little eddies and ripples in some overlooked pool of the market. There in the shade of the mangrove trees, you might just find the next great investment idea.

SO MANY OPPORTUNITIES . . .

After 44 years, Nathu La Pass reopened. Literally translated as "the pass of the listening ear," it was part of the old Silk Road, the ancient link between India and China, between Asia and Europe. After a border war between China and India, the two nations closed Nathu La Pass in 1962, ending the mule-laden trade between the two.

Though somewhat restricted, trading began again in yak tails, goatskins, tea, rice, flour, clothes, shoes, blankets, kerosene, and tobacco. Undoubtedly, the mule trains will again make the trek through the rugged vista—jagged mountains, whipping wind, and arid air.

Symbolically, it was a sign of more open trade between the two regional rivals. I love stories like this. They show how the world continues to change, in small and big ways. The opening of this stretch of the old Silk Road is a good metaphor for the opening of new passageways in the global economy. So many opportunities, so much potential. It will be fascinating to watch.

I hope this book inspires you in some way and informs your decision-making in new ways. May you prosper in whatever markets you find yourself in!

NOTES

CHAPTER 1: A TALE OF TWO MARKETS

1. Henry Clews, *Twenty-eight Years in Wall Street* (New York: J. S. Ogilvie, 1887).
2. Adam Smith, *Supermoney* (Hoboken, NJ: John Wiley & Sons, 2006), p. xxvii.
3. Benjamin Graham, *The Intelligent Investor*, rev. ed., with new commentary by Jason Zweig (New York: HarperBusiness Essentials, 2003), p. 203.
4. Martin J. Whitman and Martin Shubik, *The Aggressive Conservative Investor* (Hoboken, NJ: John Wiley & Sons), p. 256.
5. Graham and Zweig, *The Intelligent Investor*, rev. ed., p. 203.
6. John Burr Williams, *The Theory of Investment Value* (1930; reprint, Burlington, VT: Fraser Publishing, 1997), p. 11.
7. Ibid., p. 12.
8. Seth A. Klarman, *Margin of Safety: Risk-Averse Value Investing Strategies for the Thoughtful Investor* (New York: HarperCollins, 1991), p. 11.
9. Ibid., p. 9.
10. Ibid., p. 106.
11. Ibid., p. 107.
12. Louis Lowenstein, *Sense and Nonsense in Corporate Finance* (Boston: Addison-Wesley, 1991), p. 123.
13. John Train, *Dance of the Money Bees: A Professional Speaks Frankly on Investing* (Burlington, VT: Fraser Publishing, 2000), p. 139.
14. Chris Mayer, "Concrete Slabs with 300% Profit Margins," *Capital & Crisis*, no. 13 (March 2005).

15. Graham and Zweig, *The Intelligent Investor*, rev. ed., p. 391.

16. Ibid., p. 390.

17. Ibid., p. 393.

CHAPTER 2: THE DEALMAKER'S TOOLBOX

1. Philip L. Carret, *A Money Mind at Ninety* (Burlington, VT: Fraser Publishing, 1991), p. 4.

2. *Poor Charlie's Almanack: The Wit and Wisdom of Charles T. Munger*, Peter D. Kaufman, ed. (Marceline, MO: Walsworth Publishing, 2005), p. 177.

3. Ibid., p. 45.

4. Eric Heyman, "Chairman's Message to Shareholders of the Olstein Financial Alert Fund, August 26, 2005," available at: http://www.olsteinfunds .com/TOFAF-Annual05.pdf (accessed June 4, 2007).

5. Klarman, *Margin of Safety*, p. 90.

6. Benjamin Graham and David Dodd, *Security Analysis* (New York: McGraw-Hill, 1934), p. 55.

7. Quoted in Benjamin Graham, *The Intelligent Investor* (New York: Harper & Row, 1973), p. 300.

8. Klarman, *Margin of Safety*, p. 93.

9. Ibid., p. 94.

10. Jesse Eisinger, "Lear Case Shows Sometimes Investors Can Detect Crises before Management," *Wall Street Journal*, March 15, 2006.

11. George Muzea, *The Vital Few versus the Trivial Many: A Unique Concept for Always Making Money in the Stock Market* (Newport Beach, CA: Literary Press, 2003), p. 29.

12. Charles Bukowski, "a flashing of the odds," *The Last Night of the Earth Poems* (New York: Ecco, 1992). Reprinted by permission of HarperCollins Publishers.

13. James Tisch, "Keynote Address to the Ninth Annual Columbia Investment Management Conference," Columbia University, New York, February 3, 2006.

14. Klarman, *Margin of Safety*, p. 110.

15. Chris Mayer, "More Than Just Manure," *Capital & Crisis*, no. 12 (February 2005).

CHAPTER 3: CREATING WEALTH—OR WHAT MAKES STOCKS RISE

1. Josef Penso de la Vega, *Confusión de Confusiónes*, in *Extraordinary Popular Delusions and the Madness of Crowds and Confusión de Confusiónes*, Martin Fridson, ed. (Hoboken, NJ: Wiley, 1996), pp. 162–163.

2. Ibid., p. 166.

3. Martin J. Whitman, *Value Investing: A Balanced Approach* (New York: John Wiley & Sons, 2001), p. 53. Reprinted with permission of John Wiley & Sons, Inc.
4. Ibid., p. 101.
5. Ibid., p. 103.
6. Ibid.
7. Ibid.
8. Ibid., p. 107.
9. Klarman, *Margin of Safety*, p. 124.

CHAPTER 4: HUNTING GROUNDS

1. Frederick Lewis Allen, *Since Yesterday: The Nineteen-Thirties in America, September 3, 1929–September 3, 1939* (New York: Harper Perennial, 1972), p. 182.
2. Ibid., p. 183.
3. Ibid., p. 184.
4. Ibid.
5. F. J. Chu, *The Mind of the Market: Spiritual Lessons for the Active Investor* (Burlington, VT: Fraser Publishing, 1999), p. 5.
6. Barton Biggs, *Hedgehogging* (Hoboken, NJ: John Wiley & Sons, 2006), p. 216.
7. Ibid., p. 217.
8. Joel Greenblatt, *You Can Be a Stock Market Genius Even if You're Not Too Smart: Uncover the Secret Hiding Places of Stock Market Profits* (New York: Simon & Schuster, 1997), p. 61.
9. Ibid., pp. 60–61.
10. Klarman, *Margin of Safety*, p. 191.
11. Ibid., p. 199.
12. Hilary Rosenberg, *The Vulture Investors* (Hoboken, NJ: John Wiley & Sons, 2001), p. 7.
13. Ibid., p. 16.
14. Ian M. Cumming and Joseph S. Steinberg, "Letter to Shareholders from the Chairman and President, Leucadia National Corporation, New York, 2005," available at: http://www.leucadia.com/C&P%20Letters/C&P2004.pdf (accessed June 7, 2007).
15. Ibid.
16. Frederick Lewis Allen, *The Big Change: America Transforms Itself, 1900–1950* (New York: Harper & Brothers, 1952).
17. James Montier, "Global Equity Strategy: Improving Returns Using Inside Information" (London and Frankfurt: Dresdner Kleinwort Securities, November 30, 2006).
18. Jim Rogers, *Hot Commodities: How Anyone Can Invest Profitably in the World's Best Market* (New York: Random House, 2004), pp. 178–179.

CHAPTER 5: THE CRACKS AND CREVICES OF INVESTMENT WISDOM

1. Jonathan Grotenstein and Storms Reback, *All In: The (Almost) Entirely True Story of the World Series of Poker* (New York: Thomas Dunne Books, 2005), p. 36.
2. Ibid., p. 37.
3. Ibid., p. 48.
4. Ibid., p. 35.
5. Michael J. Mauboussin, *More Than You Know: Finding Financial Wisdom in Unconventional Places* (New York: Columbia University Press, 1996), p. 17.
6. Ibid., p. 17.
7. Michael J. Mauboussin, "Mauboussin on Strategy: How Do You Compare?" *Legg Mason Capital Management Newsletter*, August 9, 2006.
8. Murray Stahl, *Collected Commentaries and Conundrums Regarding Value Investing: The Essays of Murray Stahl* (Seattle: Horizon Asset Management, 1998), p. 100.
9. Ibid., pp. 43–44.
10. Ron Muhlencamp, *Harvesting Profits on Wall Street* (Wexford, PA: Muhlenkamp & Co., 2006), p. 27.
11. Ibid., p. 95.
12. Jonathan Davis, *Investing with Anthony Bolton: The Anatomy of a Stock Market Phenomenon* (Hampshire, UK: Harriman House, 2004), p. 18.
13. James Grant, "Value at Risk," *Grant's Interest Rate Observer*, vol. 24, no. 21 (November 3, 2006).
14. Whitman and Shubik, *The Aggressive Conservative Investor*, p. 17.
15. Ibid., p. 256.
16. Ralph Wanger, "Report to Stockholders: Columbia Acorn 2004 Annual Report," available at: http://www.secinfo.com/dr6sj.zTq.htm.
17. All subsequent quotes from Ralph Wanger are from this interview with the author, Chicago, May 2005.
18. Humphrey B. Neill, *The Art of Contrary Thinking* (Caldwell, ID: Caxton Printers, 1992), page 1.
19. Michael Panzner, *The New Laws of the Stock Market Jungle: An Insider's Guide to Successful Investing in a Changing World* (Upper Saddle River, NJ: Financial Times Prentice Hall, 2004.), page 45.
20. Charles D. Ellis, *Winning the Loser's Game* (New York: McGraw-Hill, 2004), p. 9.
21. Ibid., p. 24.
22. Robert A. Olstein, "Chairman's Message to Shareholders of the Olstein Financial Alert Fund, August 26, 2005," available at: http://www.olsteinfunds.com/TOFAF-Annual05.pdf (accessed June 4, 2007).
23. Ibid.
24. "Renaissance Investor" (profile of Bill Miller), *Value Investor Insight*, June 19, 2005.

25. Ibid.
26. Roy R. Neuberger, *So Far, So Good: The First 94 Years* (Hoboken, NJ: John Wiley & Sons, 2001), p. 165.
27. Ibid., p. 167.
28. Ibid., p. 170.
29. Ibid., p. 176.
30. Ibid., p. 183.
31. John Neff, with S. L. Mintz, *John Neff on Investing* (Hoboken, NJ: John Wiley & Sons, 1999), p. 83.
32. Ibid., p. 101.
33. Louis Lowenstein, "Searching for Rational Investors in a Perfect Storm," Columbia Law and Economics working paper 255 (October 4, 2004), available at: SSRN: http://ssrn.com/abstract=625123 or DOI: 10.2139/ssrn.625123.
34. Ibid.
35. Ibid.
36. Davis, *Investing with Anthony Bolton*, p. 57.
37. Ibid., p. 20.
38. Ibid., p. 31.
39. Ibid.
40. Ibid., p. 25.
41. Ibid., p. 67.
42. Ibid., p. 75.
43. Ibid., p. 67.
44. Smith, *Supermoney*, p. xxviii.
45. The Fairholme Fund web site, introduction, www.fairholmefunds.com.
46. Daniel Fisher, "Mr. Big," *Forbes*, March 13, 2006, available at: http://members.forbes.com/global/2006/0313/024.html.
47. Ibid.
48. Christopher H. Browne, *The Little Book of Value Investing* (Hoboken, NJ: John Wiley & Sons, 2007), p. 41.
49. Ibid., p. 42.
50. Max Gunther, *The Zurich Axioms: Investment Secrets of Swiss Bankers* (New York: Signet, 1985), p. xiii.
51. Ibid., p. 88.
52. Ibid., p. 75.
53. Ibid., p. 82.
54. Ibid., p. 90.
55. Ibid., p. 91.
56. Eric D. Beinhocker, *Origin of Wealth: Evolution, Complexity, and the Radical Remaking of Economics* (Boston: Harvard Business School Press, 2006), p. 348.
57. Mark Tier, *The Winning Investment Habits of Warren Buffett & George Soros* (New York: St. Martin's Press, 2005), p. 110.
58. Ibid., p. 139.

59. Jack Schwager, *Market Wizards* (New York: New York Institute of Finance, 1989), p. 286.
60. Tier, *Becoming Rich*, p. 151.
61. Ibid., p. 220.
62. Ibid., p. 224.

CHAPTER 6: WHEN TO SELL

1. Graham, *The Intelligent Investor*, p. 206.
2. Grant, "When to Sell."
3. Ibid.
4. Ibid.

CHAPTER 7: ON DOING THE WRONG THING

1. Charles Nicholl, *The Fruit Palace: An Odyssey through Colombia's Cocaine World* (New York: St. Martin's Press, 1985).
2. Ibid.
3. Martin T. Sosnoff, *Humble on Wall Street* (New Rochelle, NY: Arlington House, 1975), p. 9.
4. Quoted in ibid., p. 14.
5. Ibid., p. 15.
6. Ibid., p. 68.
7. Ibid., p. 69.
8. Ibid.
9. Ibid., p. 76.
10. Ilan Stavans, *Dictionary Days* (St. Paul, MN: Graywolf Press, 2005), p. 150.
11. John Emerich Edward Dalberg-Acton, "The Rise and Fall of the Mexican Empire," in *Selected Writings of Lord Action*, vol. 2, J. Rufus Frears, ed. (Indianapolis: Liberty Fund, 1986).
12. Douglas Adams, *The Hitchhiker's Guide to the Galaxy* (New York: Ballantine Books, 2002), p. 105.
13. Ibid., p. 102.
14. Ibid.
15. Ibid., p. 16.
16. Emanuel Derman, *My Life as a Quant: Reflections on Physics and Finance* (Hoboken, NJ: John Wiley & Sons, 2004), p. 267.
17. Ibid., p. 28.
18. Edward Chancellor and Marathon Asset Management, *Capital Account: A Money Manager's Reports from a Turbulent Decade, 1993–2002* (New York: Thomson/Texere, 2004), p. 21.

19. Seth Klarman, "2006 Year-End Letter" (Boston: Baupost Value Partners, LP, The Baupost Group, LLC).

20. Leon Cooperman, "Keynote Address to the 10th Annual Columbia Investment Management Conference," Columbia University, New York, February 2, 2007.

21. Max Gunther, *The Luck Factor: Why Some People Are Luckier Than Others and How You Can Become One of Them* (New York: Macmillan, 1977), p. 62.

22. Ibid.

23. Ibid., p. 63.

CHAPTER 8: SMALL QUESTIONS, BIG OPPORTUNITIES

1. Anthony Bourdain, *The Nasty Bits,* New York: Bloomsbury, 2006. Reprinted by permission of Bloomsbury USA.

INDEX